D1277080

Studies in
Writing & Rhetoric

IN 1980, THE CONFERENCE ON COLLEGE COMPOSITION AND COM-
munication perceived a need for providing publishing opportunities
for monographs that were too long for publication in its journal and
too short for the typical scholarly books published by The National
Council of Teachers of English. The Studies in Writing and Rhetoric
series was conceived, and a Publications Committee established.

Monographs to be considered for publication may be speculative,
theoretical, historical, analytical, or empirical studies; research re-
ports; or other works contributing to a better understanding of composition and communication, including interdisciplinary studies or
studies in related disciplines. The SWR series will exclude textbooks,
unrevised dissertations, book-length manuscripts, course syllabi,
lesson plans, and collections of previously published material.

Any teacher-writer interested in submitting a work for publication in this series should submit either a prospectus and sample
manuscript or a full manuscript to the NCTE Director of Publications, 1111 Kenyon Road, Urbana, IL 61801. Accompanied by sample
manuscript, a prospectus should contain a rationale, a definition of
readership within the CCCC constituency, comparison with related
extant publications, a tentative table of contents, and an estimate of
length in double-spaced 8½ × 11 sheets and the date by which full
manuscript can be expected. Manuscripts should be in the range of
100 to 170 typed manuscript pages.

The present work serves as a model for future SWR monographs.

Paul O'Dea
NCTE Director of Publications

A New Perspective on Cohesion in Expository Paragraphs

Robin Bell Markels

WITH A FOREWORD BY MIRIAM T. CHAPLIN

Published for Conference on College
Composition and Communication

SOUTHERN ILLINOIS UNIVERSITY PRESS
Carbondale and Edwardsville

To the memory of my teacher, Dudley Hascall,
who inspired this work, and to my husband,
Julian Markels, who sustained it.

Production of works in this series has been partly funded by the Conference on College Composition and Communication of the National
Council of Teachers of English.

Printed in the United States of America
Designed by Design for Publishing, Inc., Bob Nance
Production supervised by Kathleen Giencke

Library of Congress Cataloging in Publication Data

Markels, Robin Bell.
  A new perspective on cohesion in expository paragraphs.

  (Studies in writing and rhetoric)
  "Published for Conference on College Composition and
Communication."
  Bibliography: p.
  1. English language—Paragraphs.   2. English language—
Noun.   3. English language—Discourse analysis.
  4. Exposition (Rhetoric)   I. Conference on College
Composition and Communication.   II. Title.   III. Series.
  PE1439.M28   1984   425   83-14561
  ISBN 0-8093-1152-6

Contents

Foreword

Miriam T. Chaplin

PROBABLY THE MOST COMMON CRITICISM THAT ENGLISH TEACHers make of students' writing is that it lacks cohesion. The comment often causes a great deal of confusion. Yet, when students read, they are quite aware that a written selection is not clear when the writer has failed to string ideas together so that there is continuity and logic. It is possible that the difficulty that students experience in grasping the concept of cohesion stems from its abstract quality. While cohesion is the essence of written language, its identity is not specifically restricted to a particular word or phrase. Metaphorically, cohesion is like the seasoning in a favorite dish. It increases the appeal, excites the intellectual appetite, and provides distinction for the writer's attempt to explain a fact or tell a story. Without cohesion, the reader is lost in a labyrinth of ideas, stumbling about in search of a meaningful release to no avail.

Rhetoricians have generally conceived of cohesion, unity, and emphasis as a triumvirate firmly embedded in the deep structure of a writer's ideas. In this text, Robin Markels goes one step further and asserts that cohesion exists in a superordinate relationship to unity and emphasis and must be considered a part of the surface structure of written language as well as the deep structure. Confining her investigation to expository paragraphs, she identifies cohesion as the quality which imparts meaning through the use of nouns strategically placed, synonomized, or implied by the writer. She maintains that the repetition of a single term gives a paragraph semantic consistency, and the appearance of that term in a conspicuous subject position provides syntactic consistency.

Her discussion, however, does not ignore the reader. Without compromising the importance of the text, she emphasizes the contribution that the reader makes to the text's fulfillment. Indeed, she implies that the message of the text cannot exceed the reader's world view. There are textual cues which cement the words into a meaningful whole, and there are cues of experience which must be shared between the reader and the writer. It is this "path of connection between unique and discrete individuals" which allows the reader to experience cohesion as the reading process unfolds.

Traditionally, a paragraph is defined as the development of one idea. It is expected that a writer will introduce an idea and support it in a variety of ways. The main idea may be stated or implied; it may control related ideas, or it may lead to the development of other ideas. According to Markels, the complexity of the paragraph structure determines its character. She analyzes paragraphs which employ single term chains, double chains, and mixed chains. Furthermore, these techniques of discourse are not bound to a topic or base sentence. Markels states that the "functional, structural, and informational necessity for a topic sentence . . . depends primarily on the informational purpose of the message." Cohesion is the result of a consistency in paragraph structure rather than a reliance on a particular structure.

So much of the writing in linguistics texts is coherent only to linguists. This text represents a refreshing departure from that tradition. Though it certainly contains important information for persons concerned with the science of language, it is also a valuable commentary on the paragraph as a basic unit of written language. The approach that Markels takes and the relaxed style that she embraces make this text readable for a wide audience, and it will be especially appealing to those who write and teach the universe of discourse.

The analysis of the structure underlying paragraph formation as explained by Markels provides tangible models that teachers can use in teaching cohesion to students. Furthermore, an understanding of these models does not require extensive knowledge of grammar. Thus, explanations can be given to student writers at various stages of development. Most importantly, the progression of Markels' presentation from simple to complex structures provides an inherent pedagogical format easily adaptable to instructional plans. Finally, the rigidity of the models gives teachers and students an objective

means of editing and evaluating paragraphs to determine their cohesiveness without the threat of favoritism for one writer's style
over another's. For all of these reasons, Robin Markels has made an
outstanding contribution to the field of writing instruction.

Rutgers University
Camden, New Jersey

1

Basic Notions

ALL USERS OF LANGUAGE HAVE AN INTUITIVE UNDERSTANDING about what constitutes cohesive discourse. Whether listening to a lecture or reading a text, a person looks for meaningful relationships among sentences and will accept or reject a sentence sequence depending on the visibility and adequacy of those relationships. With necessary and appropriate relationships, a text achieves cohesion and "makes sense." The purpose of this analysis is to formalize some of this innate knowledge about discourse by describing some of the textual cues that contribute to cohesion in particular types of English paragraphs. The principal topic of investigation is the semantic relations among nouns necessary to create noun chains, and the syntactic information necessary to invest those chains with cohesion, in expository paragraphs.

Because cohesion does impart sense and meaning to a text, researchers have treated it as an almost exclusively semantic phenomenon. Halliday and Hasan write: "We can interpret cohesion . . . as the set of semantic resources for linking a SENTENCE with what has gone before."[1] The basis for linking is the sharing of a referent, which Halliday and Hasan call a "tie," and studies by Witte and Faigley report a high correlation between well-written student texts and the number of ties employed.[2] However, as Witte and Faigley also report, the "tie theory" does not offer a means for explaining sentence sequences that contain ties but nevertheless lack cohesion, as in the following example:

John likes *oranges. Oranges* grow in California. Roscoe throws *oranges* at the referees of basketball games. *Oranges* and apples are fruit.

Instead of assuming cohesion to be an exclusively semantic relation, my analysis demonstrates that it is both semantic and syntactic, and provides a methodology for specifying the necessary conditions for *textual* cohesion in particular paragraph types. While noun chains establish semantic consistency, only the interaction of those chains with the syntactic information that thematizes them can create cohesion.

In analyzing the contribution of syntax to cohesion, the analysis depends primarily on surface structure grammar, since it is surface grammar that most nearly captures an author's actual discourse decisions about theme and thematic development. In using this approach, the analysis challenges the currently popular deep structure approaches to cohesion and comprehension typified by the work of Walter Kintsch and his associates.[3] These approaches essentially deconstruct texts into strings of propositions—two-term statements similar to the "kernel sentences" of transformational grammar—and in that process, obliterate textual craftsmanship and the grammatical and thematic relationships on which that craftsmanship depends: subordination, coordination, and complementation. Ultimately these approaches offer no means by which to synthesize the elements of a text, to describe textual totality, or to account for our intuitive sense of a textual whole that is greater than the sum of its parts.

The textual whole that will form the basis for my analysis is the English paragraph, and I assume that in describing some of the relationships between nouns and noun chains in paragraphs, I am also describing some of the basic discourse structures from which paragraphs are made. My description leads to a new, structural classification of paragraph types, and it offers additional evidence that the paragraph is an identifiable structure within a shared, public grammar of discourse, rather than a mere agglomerate produced by artificial convention or authorial whimsy. Despite evidence to the contrary, the conception of the paragraph as an arbitrary indentation still dominates the work of rhetoricians and composition teachers, and this conception remains an obstacle both to further research and to effective teaching.

My analysis begins with a justification for using the term "cohesion" to describe most fully the qualities we associate with a coherent text. "Cohesion" is presented as a superordinate term embracing both "unity" and "coherence," and is defined as the presence of a dominant term, either directly or inferentially, in each sentence of a paragraph. Chapter 2 concludes with the hypothesis that the textual patterning of a dominant term creates in rudimentary form a structural whole or totality. Whereas chapter 2 examines cohesion as inherent in the text, chapter 3 examines cohesion from the reader's perspective and summarizes recent psycholinguistic research that supports the hypothesis developed in chapter 2. In chapters 4 and 5, the definition of cohesion as a dominant term present in each sentence of a paragraph, and whose recurrences manifest a structural totality, is developed through a variety of paragraphs, specifically paragraphs in which structure is defined by a single-term chain, a double-term chain, and a mixed chain. The essay concludes by suggesting briefly the implications of my analysis both for the theory of discourse and the teaching of composition.

2

The Cohesive Paragraph

ON AN ORDINARY, DAY-TO-DAY LEVEL, PEOPLE EQUATE COHESION with the simple and sustaining fact that some sentence sequences make sense and others do not. Cohesion elevates a random collection of sentences to the status of a text, and in the process imparts meaning, insight, and purpose to those sentences. Without cohesion, the text can hardly be said to exist at all, for cohesion provides the textual means for initiating comprehension or sense.

Since that description attributes to cohesion the survival of civilization, the maintenance of friends, lovers, marriage, and peace, not to mention the successful preparation of a Stouffer's spinach souffle or a simple paragraph, some clarification of the term, as distinct from the traditional unity and coherence, seems appropriate.

An ordinary reader would, I trust, think the following passage incoherent:

> A fresh batch of cheese is received at Mjuller's store. The best adornment for a maid is modesty and a transparent dress. At sunset wild ducks flew over the little cradle. They're waiting for you at the meeting of the municipal government, Mr. Lancelot.[1]

The passage does not make sense: in the absence of a single subject, it lacks unity; in the absence of logical order among statements, or of individual words linking statements together, it lacks coherence; and in its overall failure to become a comprehensible text, it lacks what I am calling cohesion. At this level cohesion represents the first and most basic condition of any text because it differentiates a meaningful sequence of sentences from a mere agglomerate. This usage is compatible with our intuitive understanding of the term but does differ from the rhetoricians' "coherence." In their usage, coherence is one of three equally important qualities—along with unity and emphasis—which together constitute a text. I am using cohesion as a superordinate term embracing all three qualities and in the following section will try to justify that usage. I review the main characteristics of unity and coherence as traditionally understood, and try to show how both in fact are components of cohesion.

The division of labor between coherence and unity probably had no specific historical origin. Rhetoricians distinguished the two, of course, but the real heritage of the distinction derives from Alexander Bain's influential *English Composition and Rhetoric,* 1877. In his famous chapter on the paragraph, Bain prescribed a set of six rules for achieving good paragraphs. The first required that "the bearing of each sentence upon what went before be explicit and unmistakable," or, in traditional terms, exhibit coherence.[2] The fifth rule required a paragraph to possess unity, which "implies a definite purpose, and forbids digressions and irrelevant matter."[3]

As generally understood, these two rules ascribe singleness of subject matter to unity, and to coherence the orderly arrangement of the unified material; more recent scholars maintain Bain's distinction:

> A thing is unified if its parts relate to some over-arching principle informing the whole. It is coherent if its parts—especially adjacent parts—are fixed in their relationships to one another. A handful of marbles has unity; but they have no coherence, as one may easily prove by trying to bounce them as one piece across the floor. On the other hand, a piece of sticky bubble gum and a marble may show coherence, but they won't show unity, at least not if they were brought together without principle. . . . Unity and coherence are thus independent variables.[4]

If we can regard unity provisionally as the development of a central or single idea, we can look more closely at the attributes of coherence, a considerably more difficult concept to pin down, even descriptively. Some definitions offer a starting point. James Mc-Crimmon writes: "A paragraph is said to have coherence when its sentences are woven together or flow into one another."[5] Echoing McCrimmon, Hodges and Whitten advise: "Give coherence to the paragraph by so interlinking the sentences that the thought may flow from one sentence to the next."[6] Others interpret coherent, "flowing" sentences as orderly sentences. Charles Ruhl: "I will consider discourse to be coherent if there are logical relations between its parts."[7] H. B. Lathrop: "Orderly sequence is coherence."[8] And finally, Lybbert and Cummings elaborate on McCrimmon's quality of "woven together": "A minimal definition of coherence might be 'fixed interdependence and non-autonomy of parts.'"[9]

What emerges from these descriptions and definitions is the simple idea that linking sentences together generates coherence and that to attain that linkage, authors need to repeat words or establish equivalence chains of meaning:

Link sentences together by means of pronouns referring to antecedents in preceding sentences.[10]

Link sentences by repeating words or ideas used in preceding sentences.[11]

By repeating key words and phrases, a writer can keep the dominant subject in the reader's mind and maintain the kind of continuity necessary for a smooth flow of logical thought.[12]

Implicit in this advice to repeat words to create coherence is really the advice to create unity. Despite the premise that the two are separate qualities, at least one aspect of coherence involves unity. If there is no "dominant subject," if there are no "key phrases to repeat," then unity as well as coherence is missing. The distinction between unity and coherence is not so easily maintained; they do not turn out to be independent variables, as Lybbert and Cummings argued; rather, coherence is a function of unity, as seen in the following primitive but cohesive paragraph, where the mere repetition of "fluorite" establishes simultaneously the unity of a dominant idea and cohesion:

Fluorite in commercial quantities occurs in both sedimentary and igneous rocks. Veins of fluorite with quartz or calcite sometimes contain lead, copper, and zinc materials. We are the world's largest producers of fluorite, most of it in Illinois, Kentucky, Colorado, and New Mexico. Fluorite is used to produce a fluid slag in steel-making and in smelting ores. It is used in making high-test gasoline, Freon, and many other chemical products. Fluorite is a most attractive mineral of varied colors—white, blue, green, and violet.[13]

Given the way real texts actually hang together with little more than repeated nouns or themes, the concept of unity becomes the basis for a minimal but at least somewhat operational definition of cohesion, as proposed by Irena Bellert and Walter Kintsch:

> A necessary (though obviously not sufficient) condition of the coherence of a text consists, roughly speaking, in repetitions. The . . . structure of each utterance S_1 of a text $S_1, \ldots , S_n$ is such that at least one lexical item which occurs in it, or one proposition which can be inferred from it, can also be found within the utterances of the sequences $S_1, \ldots S_{i-1}$, or within the propositions which can be inferred from those.[14]

> We suggest a text base is cohesive if it is connected by argument repetition.[15]

Unity Through Recurrence Chains

The first level of cohesion, then, is the recurrence of the same lexical item. The simplest form of this recurrence is the repetition of the same term in which a strict identity relationship is upheld, as in:

The boys climbed the *trees*. The *trees* weren't too tall for them.

Frequently, however, strict identity is not required, even when the terms are ultimately morphologically the same, as in:

I wanted to buy some *apples*. But *they* were sold out.

Take care of your *wallet*. Peter always tries to pick *it* from his closest friends.[16]

In these examples, the apples to be purchased are not identical to those sold out, nor is John's wallet identical to the ones picked. One must posit a kind of existential class of apples or wallets in which both terms represent subsets of their respective classes; instead of the relation of identity, the terms exhibit one of class membership.

A third kind of recurrence is synonymy: items which share the same referent and which can be substituted for one another without significantly changing the meaning, as in:

The *boy* climbed the fence. The *youth* is a member of a gang.

This general and commonplace notion of synonymy would outrage philosophers; in their view, no two words will be identical in all contexts and thus synonymy is impossible. Yet since almost all texts consistently exploit synonymy for stylistic variation, any practical discourse analysis must either rely on this subjective definition or must be abandoned.

Additionally, a text signals repetitions with items that are equivalent—similar—rather than identical. In some instances, there is no clear distinction between synonymy and equivalence, which causes some authors to group them together. I am separating them on the ground that synonymy involves the same referent, but that equivalence involves a class-member referent as in the apples and wallets examples. Like synonymy, equivalence is an intuitive concept that resists formal definition; having no sufficiently rigorous semantic theory for equivalence, we must again rely on rough, ready, and usually subjective notions of similarity. Some potential kinds of equivalence are the following suggested by Enkvist:

contracting hyponymy: *People* got on and off. At the newstand *Frenchmen*, returning to Paris, bought that day's paper.

expanding hyponymy: *Tulips* are cheap even in January. But then *flowers* seem to be necessary to Scandinavians during the darkest season.

sustained metaphor: The sun *sagged* yellow over the grass plots and bruised itself on the clotted cotton fields. The fertile countryside that grew things in other seasons spread flat from the roads and lay *prone* in ribbed fans of broken discouragement.

co-membership of the same world field: *Tulips* are cheap. *Roses* are expensive.[17]

As this classification suggests, categorizing the semantic relation between words is a very problematic venture. One also needs, for example, a system that describes the cohesive effect of a sequence like:

The *girls* played house. The *boys* spit on them. In all, the *children* were feisty that day.

Here *boys* and *girls*, since they are opposites, cannot share the same referent, but as members of a class they share the textual antecedent "children." Given the breadth and complexity of these relations, equivalence can best be defined as items exhibiting set-relations with one another. This evasive definition echoes those reached by other researchers. Halliday, in "The Linguistic Study of Texts," defines equivalence as "two or more occurrences, in close proximity, of the same lexical item, or of items paradigmatically related in the sense that they may belong to the same lexical set."[18] Halliday uses the example "I took leave and turned to the ascent of the peak. The climb was perfectly easy." Similarly, Winburne, in his analysis of the Gettysburg Address, defines equivalence as items belonging to the "same semantic class," and groups in "one semantic class the items *here* and *battlefield*."[19]

Although we lack a full and detailed articulation, these three categories of (1) item repetition, with either complete or partial identity, (2) synonymy, and (3) equivalence do enable us to trace Bellert's repetitions (or what I am calling item recurrences) in patterns through a text, even when the recurrences are not literal. A text's ordinary use of repetition/substitution/variation, as it develops and refines its topic, requires such an approach. Additionally, using these three categories to indicate an item's relation to its referent enables a researcher to estimate the cohesiveness of a recurrence chain by asking whether the repeated items all stand in the same relation to their shared antecedent/referent. Thus the cohesiveness of the following sequence can be attributed to tulips' and daisies' shared relationship to flowers as members of a class:

Tulips are cheap in January. Daisies are plentiful also. But then flowers seem to be necessary to Swedes.

On the other hand, the following sequence lacks cohesiveness because "dogs" and "tulips" do not share an identifiable relationship to
"flowers" as their common antecedent/referent:

> Tulips are cheap in January. Dogs are plentiful, too. But then
> flowers seem to be necessary to Swedes.

Second, these three categories provide a means for determining
the cohesiveness of recurrences that are implied rather than stated.
If no antecedent/referent is stated, but if one can be inferred to
which all recurring items stand in the same relation, then the sequence can be perceived as cohesive:

> The gearbox was smoking. The windshield wipers were stuck.

Here "gearbox" and "wipers" both stand in part-whole relation to
the implied referent, "car."
  Finally, the categories provide a means for distinguishing between strongly and weakly cohesive passages. The more narrowly
the implied antecedent/referent is specified, the more strongly cohesive the sequence will be. Thus the following passage would receive low marks for cohesion:

> Tulips are cheap in January. Shrubs are plentiful, too. But then
> flowers seem necessary to Swedes.

The implied referent has to be some highly general term like
"plants," which designates too broad a class to establish clear equivalence among tulips, flowers, and shrubs.
  In summary, then, recurrences establish unity where two or more
recurring items—what I am calling a recurrence chain—enable a
text to develop its basic topic by a series of substitutions in which
there may be an interplay between lexical repetition, synonymy,
and equivalence.
  Besides these three semantic means for creating recurrences,
texts also employ grammatical means: substitution, reference, and
ellipsis. All basically abbreviations for the just discussed lexical recurrences, these methods are quite straightforward and considerably less problematic than the lexical recurrences. Halliday and
Hasan, in *Cohesion in English*, exhaustively describe and analyze
these methods; in brief summary, they are as follows. Substitution

is "the replacement of one item by another," as in "My *axe* is too blunt. I must get a sharper *one.*"[20] Reference involves items that cannot be understood in their own right and must be interpreted by their antecedents:[21] personal references indicated by *he, she, him,* and the like; demonstrative references indicated by *this, these, those,* and the like; and comparative references indicated by *better, best,* and the like. Ellipsis is "the omission of an item,"[22] as in "Would you like to hear another verse? I know twelve more."[23] Since these are grammatical substitutions, and to that extent place-holders for lexical items, these methods are really ancillary to semantic recurrences in a cohesion study.

Cohesion and Sentence Constituents

As a means for tracking the topic of a text, recurrence chains—whether lexical or grammatical—represent a first step in describing cohesion. But recurrence chains are merely word lists, and to attain the status of discourse they must be incorporated into sentences. At this juncture a second set of relationships must be introduced: the syntactic relations of sentences and sentence constituents to one another. These relations lie in the traditional domain of coherence—the relationships between parts, with the individual sentence assigned the role of "part." Halliday and Hasan typify the traditional view: "We can interpret cohesion . . . as the set of semantic resources for linking a SENTENCE with what has gone before."[24] There are many examples where cohesion is achieved by linking entire sentences to each other:

The door slammed shut. The window blew open.

He showed no pleasure at hearing the news. Instead, he looked even gloomier.

But there are also instances where we sense that only parts of sentences are being linked with only parts of other sentences:

In joining an organization, the individual accepted a set of fixed obligations for a specified set of rewards. These obligations and rewards remained the same over a relatively long span of time.[25]

With a little tinkering, we can accentuate this sense of parts linked to parts:

> In joining an organization, the individual accepted a set of obligations in return for a set of rewards. The obligations were fixed. The rewards were specified. These obligations and rewards remained the same over a relatively long span of time.

In the same way, we can often condense into one sentence the previously linked parts of two sentences:

> The hustlers have co-opted every salable affliction. This bothers me.

> The hustlers' co-opting of every salable affliction bothers me.

Because of a kind of semantic drag created by item repetition, whole sentences are often linked together as traditionally claimed; but as we know, the sentence is a very elastic unit, with no syntactic limits to its length or complexity once the minimal requirements of subject and predicate have been met, so that a SENTENCE can itself lack cohesion when relationships among constituents are unclear and meaning becomes ambiguous. And a unit that is not certain to be cohesive in itself cannot become the basis for a theory of cohesion. In fact, any sentence provides two distinct structural arrangements of semantic information: at one level, it presents information as a complete unit (the arrangement that Halliday and Hasan assume); but at a second level—the level at which sentences can lack cohesion—it presents that information as a structured array of internal elements. English is a language of synthesis and a language of position: meaning, emphasis, and theme all depend upon position, and only a dual perspective on the sentence as a unit and a structured array of elements captures these discourse qualities. The question for a cohesion study is, Which method of describing sentences best maintains this double perspective?

Deep and Surface Constituents

The most immediate choice lies between surface and deep description. The usual distinction between surface and deep constituents is that the surface structure represents the actual textual shape and content of a sentence, and the deep structure its formal and originating kernels. Thus the sentence "John bought a ball and the ball was red" and the sentence "John bought a red ball" have the same deep structure but different surface structures. The deep structure is revealed by analysis of the sentence into its primary arguments, its actual or potential recurrence chain items. Then a series of transformations affecting these kernels links and transforms the kernels' deep structures into their surface form.

Many transformations, however, are optional; whereas a given surface structure will always yield the same deep structure, a given deep structure will not always yield the same surface structure. Because of this incommensurability between deep and surface structures, and because the surface structures represent the author's actual decision about what transformations to employ, and because these decisions reflect what is said, what is omitted, what is emphasized, the description of surface forms seems most appropriate to cohesion study. Put another way, the surface forms enable us to talk about the sentence as a unit, and also provide information about the syntactic makeup of the sentence, specifically its length and kind.

Surface forms not only allow us to maintain a double perspective on the sentence as a unit and as a structured array of elements; they also enable us to introduce into discourse analysis the traditional set of grammatical concepts: subject, predicate, and modifier. These concepts, especially subject and predicate, offer a fairly straightforward means for tracking thematic movement—or recurrence chain items—through a text. They help us identify the overall pattern established by a recurring item as it moves from subject to object position, back to subject, and so forth.

The major drawback to surface structure analysis lies in its assignment of subordinate and superordinate status to constituents. In any given context, calling "John bought a red ball" more coherent than "John bought a ball and the ball was red" presumes that the surface structure accurately reveals the hierarchy among constituents. Generally it does, as in this example, but not always: certain prepositional phrases are persistent exceptions. In the surface structure prepositions are always subordinate; in the deep structure they are superordinate and dominate other constituents. Moreover, the headwords in these prepositional phrases often become dominant recurring items in a text, as in the implied recurrence of "park" in the following sequence:

> John walked in the park. The trees were just turning color. People sat on benches and fed squirrels.

In summary, then, surface forms are obvious choices for describing the sentence as a unit and for providing classificatory information about the sentence; in addition, surface forms introduce grammatical functions that can be and are exploited for purposes of coherence. On the other hand, deep structure analysis provides a more consistent hierarchy of constituents, and a hierarchy that is often reflected in the overall discourse structure but not in the surface structure. Given these parameters, my analysis will proceed on the assumption that surface forms are valid units for analysis, and also that deep structures at certain points must be dealt with; I will use the surface forms as far as they carry us, and shift to deep structures when the analysis seems to require it. Since these methods represent two demonstrable stages of sentence analysis, it should not be surprising that one or the other should be more relevant in particular situations.

Finally, it must be noted that in cohesion, the interaction between recurring lexical items and syntax is not an interaction between equals. Where a recurrence chain exists, there is cohesion; without a chain, no cohesion. It is a rocklike condition of cohesion that any sentence sequence containing a recurrence chain, no matter how simple, raw, crude, or convoluted the sentences, will still be suggestively cohesive. Syntax can maim, twist, or obscure the relations among recurring items, but whether it can completely thwart their collective power is debatable. Does a reader "understand" "colorless green ideas" because he uses the phrase's semantics or because he interprets the phrase through the paradigm of syntax? In the analysis of cohesion, the importance of syntax is an open question.

Cohesion and Coherence

Assuming that coherence, as distinct from unity, involves both sentences' deep and surface syntactic relationships, we might now seek to establish the range of these relationships and to identify their particular contribution to overall cohesion. To this end, we will compare two texts: an "original" that is unified but weakly coherent, and a revised version with greater coherence:

The opossum has survived in definitely hostile surroundings for seventy million years. The opossum is small; it can easily find a little food, while big animals starve. The individual opossum is not very delicate; it can stand severe punishment. It "plays 'possum" when it gets into trouble. It can go without food for a long time. Many different things are food to an opossum. Traits of the opossum have a high survival value. The opossum is a survivor from the Age of Reptiles.[26]

The reasons our opossum has survived in definitely hostile surroundings for 70 million years are evident. One is his small size: small animals always find hiding places, they always find a little food, where the big ones starve. Another of its assets was its astounding fecundity: if local catastrophes left only a few survivors, it did not take long to reestablish a thriving population. Also the individual opossum is not exactly delicate: it can stand severe punishment—during which it "plays 'possum" and then scampers away—and it can go without food for a considerable time. Finally, a great many things are "food" to an opossum. Each of these traits has a high survival value, and their combination has presented the United States with a survivor from the Age of Reptiles.[27]

Perhaps the most striking difference lies in the sentence constructions. In the original, the sentences are primarily kernel sentences— short, choppy, grammatically simple—containing single propositions. In the revision, the sentences vary in grammatical complexity and contain several propositions per sentence; they "flow." Thus the sentence's surface structure—the form in which propositions, particularly recurrence chain items—contributes to coherence in a significant way. For example, the revision combines two kernel sentences from the original—"The opossum has survived for 70 million years" and "The reasons are evident"—into a single, complex sentence that signals the relationship between the two kernel sentences. Quite simply, the syntactic capacity of sentences to show relationships—complementarity, as in this example, or subordination, or coordination—can be exploited to increase coherence.

A second difference lies in the number of recurrence chains in the two versions. In the original only one chain—the opossum—is overtly signaled. In the revision two chains are signaled—the opossum, and the reasons for its survival. This number, two, is a critical if somewhat obvious criterion, since it is relationships that make for coherence, and relationships require at least *two* elements. As we shall see later, while the requirement of "two" can be fulfilled by two recurrence chains, it can also be fulfilled by a recurrence chain plus another "thing."

Recurrences make for coherence not only by their frequency but also by their physical location, and ultimately by their function. Consider the following examples:

I was accepted and started work. My experience had been chiefly derived from books. I was not prepared for the difficult period of adjustment. I soon became discouraged with myself and so dissatisfied with my job that I was on the point of quitting. My employer must have sensed this. He called me into his office and talked to me about the duties of my position and the opportunities for advancement. I realized that there was nothing wrong with me or the job and I decided to stay.

I was accepted and started work. *Until that time* my experience had been chiefly derived from books, *and unfortunately* those books had not prepared me for the difficult period of adjustment *that every inexperienced secretary must face in a new position*. *Consequently*, I soon became so discouraged with myself and so dissatisfied with the job that I was on the point of quitting. *I think* my employer must have sensed this, *for* he called me into his office and talked to me about *both* the duties of my position and the opportunities it *offered* for advancement. *That talk helped me considerably. From then on, I realized* that there was nothing wrong with me or the job *that experience could not cure*, and I decided to stay.[28]

The revision differs from the original in its greater number of localized recurrences, that is, recurrences that are positioned in adjacent sentences, make only one or two appearances, and do not form chains.

The grammatical manifestations of a recurrence chain—reference, ellipsis, and substitution—are all forms of partial repetition. In the original opossum text, the primary recurrence was the repeated word "opossum"; the revision used reference, ellipsis, and substitution as well. Functionally, these devices do two things: they maintain an unbroken chain of recurrences and thereby establish some degree of cohesion through unity; they also function—at least psychologically—to subordinate information already known or recoverable by reducing the autonomy of sentences containing that information and forcing the reader back to preceding sentences for the antecedents or other substitutions.

These grammatical means for signaling recurrence chains do not convey new semantic information; the lexical means, especially equivalence, do, and it is through their addition of semantic information that further relationships between parts are established:

Grammatical: John and Bill pick peaches. They live next door.
Lexical: John and Bill pick peaches. These troublemakers live next door.

As indicated earlier, the potential relationships between items can be seen most usefully as set-relations. In this instance, John and Bill are members of the set of troublemakers; when further recurrences are added to the chain in a cohesive text, the chain itself will instantiate a pattern of relationships such as part/whole or member/class.

Thus far we have looked at the ways in which relationships between parts manifest themselves in sentence structure, the number of recurrences, the kind of recurrences, and finally the location of recurrences. We must now look at the effect of transition words in producing coherence. This group of cohesive devices has probably attracted the greatest attention because clearly they do link whole sentences, and elaborate classificaitons have been made of the sentence relationships signaled by transition words.

Milic, for instance, has proposed the following relations between sentences: additive, initial, adversative, alternative, explanatory, illustrative, and causal.[29] Winterowd, in "The Grammar of Coherence," posits seven and only seven relationships. These are: (1) coordinate; (2) obversative; (3) causative; (4) conclusive; (5) alternative; (6) inclusive; and (7) sequential.[30] No doubt these seven exist, as Winterowd's examples and our own common sense indicate; yet there are several problems, and Winterowd's analysis carries us only so far. For one thing, his list of relationships is not exhaustive after all, as the following sequences indicate:

1. Fluorite in commercial quantities occurs in both sedimentary and igneous rocks. Veins of fluorite with quartz or calcite sometimes contain lead, copper, and zinc materials.

2. It is necessary to define intellectuals. They are all those who create, distribute, and apply culture.

3. On the station platform were Negro soldiers. They wore brown uniforms and were tall, and their faces shone.

What seems basically and sometimes inexplicably to hold these sentences together is simply repeated reference, either through actual repetition or through pronouns. Of Winterowd's seven relationships, only coordination seems a possibility, but when one inserts his coordination words, the results are quite disarming:

It is necessary to define intellectuals.

$$\left\{ \begin{array}{l} \text{Furthermore} \\ \text{And} \\ \text{Also} \end{array} \right\} \text{ they are all those who create, distribute, and apply culture.}$$

The second and more fundamental difficulty with Winterowd's system is that where the sentence relationships are implicit—which he recognizes as a possibility—they can only be implied by the lexical content of the sentences, i.e., the recurrences I have already discussed. Transitional words do not in themselves create relationships; they simply mark the relationships already existing among the lexical items. As the following example indicates, if there is not already some lexical compatibility between the words of different sentences, the mere presence of transitional words cannot establish relationships among those sentences:

The albacore are beginning to run. However, in Montana it often snows in August. That is why Freud created a revolution in the way we view the human mind. Therefore, grammar seems to be a dull subject.[31]

While the logical relationships among sentences described by Winterowd and others certainly do exist, they must be seen as secondary to a more basic set of relations, namely, "equivalence" or the sharing of a single antecedent.

A final distinction between texts that are minimally unified and texts that are truly cohesive involves the means by which the pattern of relationships is instantiated, namely, the order of appearance of the recurring items. Contrast the following two texts:

1. Troublemakers lower the attractiveness of a neighborhood and bring police cars. Bill and Peter pick peaches. These troublemakers live next door.

2. Bill and Peter pick peaches. These troublemakers live next door. Troublemakers lower the attractiveness of a neighborhood and bring police cars.

The second version is more cohesive than the first because of the way in which its recurrences are ordered. In some texts such continuity involves entire propositions rather than just the recurrence chain items themselves:

1. After the death of Saul, David ruled Israel for forty years. Once he incurred the king's anger and was driven ignominiously from court. As a shepherd lad he had lived in the hills of Judea. He had vanquished the mighty Philistine with his slingshot. The sad-faced Saul was charmed with his songs. He was the sweetest singer in all Israel.

2. David, the shepherd lad who lived in the hills of Judea, was the sweetest singer in all Israel. It was he who charmed the sad-faced Saul with his songs. It was he, too, who vanquished the mighty Philistine with his slingshot. Later he incurred the anger of Saul and was driven from court. But upon Saul's death David came back and ruled Israel for forty years.[32]

In both sets of examples, ordering is contingent on the particular pattern of relationships being instantiated by the overall text.

In summary, then, cohesion consists of unity, as manifested by a recurrence chain, and coherence, as manifested by the semantic and syntactic relations among links in that chain. Unity and coherence are manifested in a variety of ways: sentence construction, number of recurrences, location of recurrences, transition words, kinds of recurrences, and order of recurrences. Of these six, only two—sentence construction and transition words—belong to the traditional category of coherence; all the others involve recurrences and belong to unity. The implication seems to be that while unity is absolutely necessary to cohesion, the status of coherence is less clear; it may constitute essentially a refinement of unity.

Cohesion and Form

This view of coherence as a refinement of unity was strongly articulated by H. B. Lathrop in 1918, when he coined the phrase, "unity of connection," a phrase that eminently suits our perception of cohesion. Lathrop writes:

> In a word, the unity of theme, directive unity, the unity of a line, is not more truly unity than unity of connection, the unity of a chain or the unity of a woven fabric. . . . Coherence, orderliness, is simply arrangement in a systematic way, as by deduction or induction, from cause to effect, from top to bottom or from bottom to top. There is no one plan that is preeminently coherent; a coherent result is produced by any systematic principle of guidance appropriate to the case.[33]

Modern researchers echo Lathrop with similar definitions of cohesion, most of them less operational than those of Bellert and Kintsch, but definitions which attempt nevertheless to capture the interaction between unity and coherence. Geoffrey Leech writes: "Cohesion . . . is the way in which independent choices in different points of a text correspond with or presuppose one another, forming a network of sequential relations."[34]
Ross Winterowd: "If one perceives form in discourse, he also perceives coherence, for form in discourse is the internal set of consistent relationships in any stretch of discourse, whether poem, play, essay, oration, or whatever."[35] In using such phrases as "network of sequential relations" and "form in discourse," these writers, too, are trying to identify a larger, more formal kind of unity than simple unity of content, a unity that also satisfies our sense of totality or structure.
In an effort to clarify the notion of "unity of connection," the remainder of the analysis will explore and develop the following

hypothesis: cohesion consists of unity, which in turn consists of both (a) a dominating item recurrence present in or inferable from all sentences in a paragraph, and (b) a pattern or totality manifested by that item recurrence. Coherence, the orderly arrangement of recurrences, is an aspect of unity and functions to make more explicit the already present and implied relations among recurrences.

The basic difference between my definition and Bellert's lies in my additional criterion that the recurring item also "dominate" in the sentences of the paragraph. Bellert herself notes that her definition of cohesion, as basically a term shared by all sentences in a sequence, is inadequate, as seen in a passage like the following:

> John likes oranges. Oranges grow in California. Roscoe always throws oranges at the referees of basketball games. Oranges and apples are fruits. My grandmother makes orange preserves and dried orange dolls.

Although the passage contains a recurring item, oranges, it is still not cohesive, because conceptually it is not about anything; it lacks the unity of connection that can only be provided by a dominating recurrence. The concept of dominance is crucial here, and operationally defining it is the main theme of chapters 4 and 5.

A second major aspect of my hypothesis is that dominating item recurrences create or manifest a totality. I adapt the term "totality" from Jonathan Culler, who uses it to designate a form or pattern that creates a sense of wholeness: "Their [texts'] unity is produced not so much by intrinsic features of their parts as by the intent at totality of the interpretive process; the strength of the expectations which lead readers to look for certain forms of organization in a text and to find them." [36] Culler briefly suggests six possible "forms of organization": binary opposition, the dialectical resolution of a binary opposition, the displacement of an unresolved opposition by a third term, the four-term homology, the series united by a common denominator, and the series with a transcendent or summarizing final term. [37] Culler's observations parallel Kenneth Burke's, when Burke says: "Form in literature is an arousing and fulfillment of desires. A work has form in so far as one part of it leads a reader to anticipate another part, to be gratified by the sequence." [38] Burke suggests five kinds of form—progressive (subdivided into syllogistic and qualitative progression), repetitive, conventional, and minor or incidental form. The latter two need not concern us since they cover forms like the sonnet, metaphor, and apostrophe that are not directly associated with the organization of texts. Burke describes syllogistic progression as follows: "To go from A to E through B, C, and D is to obtain such form. We call it syllogistic because, given certain things, certain things must follow, the premises force the conclusion."[39]

Whereas in syllogistic progression it is a particular event, in qualitative progression it is a particular state of mind that leads through stages to another state of mind. Repetitive form, the one that most concerns us here, Burke defines as "the consistent maintaining of a principle under new guises" or the restatement of a theme by new details.[40] The extent to which these broad conceptions of form apply to paragraphs and paragraphing is a major focus of chapters 4 and 5.

These chapters will also test the hypothesis that totalities exhibiting cohesion also exhibit particular structures that can be identified and described, so that a theory of cohesion will also yield a description of paragraph structure. If an analysis of cohesion reveals the relationships among discourse parts, then it may also be expected to reveal the structure of paragraphs.

Finally, my hypothesis assumes that these large notions of totality and form are to some degree a priori, and that readers bring to the text various prior experiences that enable them to form a concept of wholeness which they expect the text to satisfy. The enormous capabilities of readers, and their contribution to cohesion, will be the subject of chapter 3.

3

The Reader and Cohesion

THE SECOND CHAPTER PRESENTED COHESION FROM A BASICALLY
text-oriented perspective and relegated the reader to a minor role.
But that is in many ways wishful thinking, since cohesion is not a
static, immanent quality of the text but rather a judgment made ultimately by the reader. The cohesiveness of a text is a matter of degree, if not taste, and what is acceptably cohesive for one reader
may very well not satisfy another. While the text is distinctly more
accessible and manageable than the reader, some note must be
taken of the reader's role and capacities. It is thus my aim in this
chapter to outline some of the facts and theories about reader cogni-
tion and information processing as these affect a text's cohesion, and
to suggest some means for incorporating the reader's role into an
analysis of cohesion. I will also indicate how the analysis of cohesion
outlined in chapter 2 seems to coincide with current theories of
listener-reader information processing.

"The reader" is probably the most fashionable research topic
around these days, one which offers work to philosophers, psychologists, linguists, artificial intelligence programmers, and literary
critics; we have Freudian, pluralistic, ideal, informed, and Norton
readers, each with different and sometimes contradictory traits,
abilities, and intelligences. Even so, all reader response theories
share one very basic and informing assumption—that the reader is
an active rather than passive processor, sharing with the author the
pragmatic assumption that a text is really a text and that it will make
sense to the reader who expects cohesion and takes for granted at

the outset that there are connections between sentences. As a result, finding cohesion becomes a teleological process in which cohesion is first assumed and then, so to speak, attained by the reader who explores the text for all possible ways in which it might be manifested.[1] The desire for cohesion is so powerful that even apparently contradictory sentences can be smoothly and logically connected by readers. Given the sequence,

> The party was a success. Bill and Mary fought.

most readers, jarred at first, quickly construct acceptable connections:

> The party was a success, even though Bill and Mary fought.

> The party was a success. Bill and Mary fought; they were funny.

In a deliberate way, the preceding example illustrates a totally commonplace phenomenon, as much taken for granted as regular breathing. No text supplies all the information necessary for its understanding; authors consistently leave out information that they feel can be inferred by the reader, so that comprehension and cohesion depend not only on linguistic cues underlying the message but also on general knowledge—"the layman's belief system concerning human behavior in Western culture"—as if the text itself were only the tip of the iceberg.[2] Freedle and Carroll illustrate this with the following example:

> Suppose Frank and Joe are walking down the street and are about to pass a hamburger stand. Frank says, "Would you like to eat here?" Such a question contains assumptions of at least time and place: The time is not "right now" but "pretty soon, after we get served," and the place is not "right here on the street" but "at the counter of the hamburger stand." Yet if Frank and Joe are walking in the park and carrying a picnic basket the question "Would you like to eat here?" would assume that the time is "right now, as soon as we can unload the basket" and the place could be "right here." In either case, the total situation supplies the context which evokes the semantic assumptions that are most consistent with the utterance.[3]

Freedle and Carroll's analysis implies a modest version of what I shall call the iceberg theory of language, in which words and sentences become tokens, lumps of coal or pieces of wampum, fragments that can be interpreted in only much larger contexts. Besides the reader's belief system about Western culture, that context also includes: the visible scene; the linguistic medium; the relationships between parties, and the specific purpose of communication.[4] These are all aspects of the larger contexts of language, or what Karl Bühler designated as "fields." Blumenthal describes Bühler's theory as follows:

> Bühler's field concept was the most important. Given two speakers of the same language, no matter how well one of them structures a sentence his utterance will fail if both parties do not share the same field to some degree. . . . There are inner aspects of the field, such as an area of knowledge, or outer aspects, such as objects in the environment. Indeed, the field can be analyzed into many aspects. The total field (Umfeld) consists not only of the practical situation (Ziegfeld) in which the utterance occurs, but also the symbol field (Symbolfeld) which is the context of language segments preceding the segment under consideration. . . . The structure of any particular language is largely field-independent, being determined by its own particular conventional rules, but the field determines how the rules are applied . . . with a "rich" external field less needs to be specified in the sentence.[5]

Bühler's field theory outlines the several perspectives guiding discourse analysis today, and prefigures the steady movement away from the conception of language as an autonomous formal entity that can be studied *in vacuo*. Whether as intellectual backlash against Chomskian rationalism or as a merely predictable pendulum swing, discourse analysis at all levels now seeks to account for the discourse pragmatics affecting language use and comprehension. Bonnie Lynn Webber, in "A Formal Approach to Discourse Anaphora," temperately concludes that: "None of the three types of anaphoric expressions that I have studied—definite anaphora, 'one'-anaphora and verb phrase anaphora—can be understood in purely linguistic terms. That is, none of them can be explained without stepping out of the language into the conceptual model each participant is synthesizing from the discourse."[6] Others, less temperate, escalate the role of discourse pragmatics. After a study of sentence memory, Bransford, Barclay, and Franks write: "In a broader sense the constructive approach argues against the tacit assumption that sentences 'carry meaning.' People carry meanings, and linguistic inputs merely act as cues which people use to recreate and modify previous knowledge of the world."[7] Language is a tool, a medium, a complicated interface between people and their world views; as an interface, a text will always include potentially more information than is explicit in its linguistic components. Yet while a text cannot be understood by attending only to its sentences, neither can it be understood without attending to those sentences. If a sentence does not carry meaning, what does it carry?

Recurrence Chains Through Inferences

Given the capacious abilities of readers to make connections between sentences and their world knowledge, and given our equally capacious ignorance about how these connections are facilitated, my discussion of reader inferences will aim at only some simple and limited generalizations for certain types of situations; more specifically, it will speak exclusively to how reader inferences often supply the recurrence chains that chapter 2 described, and it will suggest a means for incorporating reader inference into an analysis of cohesion.

In my analysis of inferencing, I have assumed Bühler's field theory—that successful communication depends on a certain amount of field overlap between author and reader—to be essentially accurate. On that assumption, the first stage of the analysis is to delimit more usefully these overlapping fields. We can begin with the following example:

John walked into the room. The chandeliers were beautiful.

On reaching the second sentence, the reader must decide which chandeliers. Since there has been no mention of chandeliers, there is no antecedent for "the chandeliers." To fill this gap, the reader builds "bridging assumptions," a term proposed by Haviland and Clark.[8] Whenever a reader cannot directly identify an antecedent, the reader "cooperates" with the author and supplies the antecedent. In this example, when the reader makes the bridging assumption that the room has chandeliers, then an inference chain or quasi syllogism connecting the two sentences might go something like this:

John came into the room. The room contained some chandeliers.
John thought the chandeliers were beautiful.[9]

The fields necessary for the reader to construct the inference chain
seem to be of three kinds, all mutually supporting each other. The
reader must first know the lexical meaning of "chandelier." Second,
the reader must have world knowledge that rooms may contain
chandeliers.[10] And finally, the reader must have discourse knowledge about the significance of the definite article. The definite article before a noun can signal at least two things: most simply, that the
noun presupposes some antecedent, and correlatively, that a noun
accompanied by a definite article can signal a relationship between
this noun and another, preceding noun, as in:

The room was filled with people. The women were . . .

John bought a new house. The front door was of massive steel.[11]

Van Dijk describes this kind of inferencing as follows: "Any individual having a specifiable relationship with an already introduced individual is PARTICULARIZED by this relation and hence definite in
surface structure."[12]

Although no single relationship is signaled by the definite article,
the fact that *some* relationship is signaled is all that is necessary.
When reaching the cue of the definite article, apparently the reader
attempts to construct a quasi syllogism, an Aristotelian enthymeme,
both from available textual information and his stored world knowledge. Even though applying discourse knowledge will not guaran-
tee the correct inference, it does apparently direct and instruct a
reader's use of world and lexical knowledge.

Yekovich and Walker, in "Identifying and Using Referents in Sentence Comprehension," report on their experiments in which subjects were tested to determine how much the use of definite articles, instead of indefinite articles, increased comprehension. Their
results indicate clearly that definite articles facilitated the identifi-
cation and use of referents.[13] Their work basically confirms observations made by Haviland and Clark, who also argued that the
definiteness of a referent affected the extent to which an antecedent
was established in memory and used to integrate new, incoming
material.[14]

In some instances, discourse knowledge, beyond directing a reader how to combine world and lexical knowledge, can also create new world knowledge; in this respect, only two of the three fields need overlap, and not all three, as Bellert, in "Solutions of the Problem of Presuppositions," has argued.[15] Given the sequence,

Picasso left. The painter went to the coast.

the reader can infer that "the painter" refers to "Picasso," even without knowing that Picasso is a painter, because of both the cueing presence of the definite article and the lexical knowledge that "Picasso" and "painter" are compatible terms sharing the feature of humanness. Indeed, authors frequently exploit this compatibility for purposes of transmitting new information. Consider the almost endless list of words that could reasonably follow "Picasso left":

The octogenarian . . .
The prize winner . . .
The screwball . . .

There can be little doubt that readers make and use such inferences constantly, and of course comprehension studies confirm this; but more interestingly, they also show that inferred propositions attain the same status in memory as explicit ones. Kintsch and Monk tested subjects who were given the following sequence:

A burning cigarette was carelessly discarded. The fire destroyed many acres of virgin forest.

After a 15-minute delay, the subjects could recall the implicit information (that the cigarette started the fire) as fast as the stated information. It is interesting and useful to note, however, that the delay in testing a subject's recall was necessary for subjects to remember the implicit information as quickly as the explicit; in recall tests done immediately after subjects read a passage, they remembered the explicit information better and faster.[16] There is obviously some virtue in being direct and explicit.

Textual Situations for Inferences

If one grants the status and function of inferred propositions, then a number of simple observations can be made about the relation of inferences to cohesion. First, if the reader is required to construct only a single premise for the completion of the enthymeme, the sequence will be more cohesive than if the reader must supply several premises. Thus the chandelier example is more cohesive than the following:

> Barbara is seventeen, and Wendy is old enough to have a driver's license too.[17]

For this sequence to be cohesive the reader would have to construct something like the following:

> Barbara is seventeen. Seventeen is old enough to have a driver's license. Barbara is old enough to have a driver's license. Wendy is seventeen. Wendy is old enough to have a driver's license too.[18]

Second, as the example suggests, if the missing premises can be constructed from terms within the text, as in the chandelier example, rather than from information outside the text, as in the driver's license example, then the sequence will be considered more cohesive.

Finally, the closer the textual antecedent is to the particularized noun, the stronger the cohesion will be. For example:

> John walked into the room. He sat down and read a magazine. Then he listened to a record. The chandelier was beautiful.

Even if the reader has accurate lexical and world knowledge about "chandelier," and does not misinterpret the sequence by assuming "chandelier" to have the same status as, say, "piano concerto" or "song," she would still not find the passage as cohesive as

> John walked into the room. The chandelier was beautiful. He read a magazine. Then he listened to a record.

Apparently because the completion of the inference chain requires the reader to leap backward over an intervening and interfering antecedent, the first sequence is less cohesive.

Several studies confirm the importance of ordering. In "Maintenance and Control in the Acquisition of Knowledge from Written Materials," by Lawrence Frase, subjects given scrambled texts were more prone to recall error than subjects given ordered texts. As good-order texts, Frase used A's are B's and B's are C's—as in the chandelier example cited just above—and as bad-order texts, he used B's are C's and A's are B's. The good-order sequence produced almost twice as many correct inferences as the bad-order.[19]

In another study by Frase, information about chess pieces was ordered in three ways: around names, i.e.,

The bishop is worth . . .

The bishop moves . . .

around attributes, i.e.,

The pawn moves . . .

The bishop moves . . .

and finally in a mixed order where neither attribute nor name was exhausted before the other was introduced. In recall tests, subjects performed best with the name order, then the attribute order, and finally the mixed order.[20]

Several hypotheses may be drawn from these findings. First, since in no case did order completely block comprehension, order must be relegated to secondary importance. This is consistent with the hypothesis in chapter 2 that unity is more important than coherence—or order—in establishing cohesion. Second, because two kinds of order were explicitly compared in the second Frase experiment, it appears that different orders can be equally cohesive and that there is no Platonic order. In this respect, another experimenter, Crothers, concluded: "It does not appear that sentence order matters—with the important qualification that only more acceptable orders are being compared."[21] Order is simply a manifestation of the particular whole or totality.

Briefly, then, we have a crude but objective means by which to measure the function of some types of inference in promoting cohesion. If a reader is required at all to construct an enthymeme from the text in order to maintain a chain of referents, then a text which requires the addition of only one premise, constructed from information within the text, and placed sequentially adjacent to the antecedent, will be more cohesive than texts not meeting those requirements.

Obviously these parameters only scratch the surface of inferencing and speak only to those inferences involving Is-A and Has-A relationships. Readers easily construct other kinds of rich infer-

ence patterns, as illustrated by Charniak's famous discussion of the
following:

> Jane was invited to Jack's birthday party. She wondered if he
> would like a kite. She went to her room and shook her piggy
> bank. It made no sound.

As Charniak points out, even young readers understand that Jane
wanted to buy Jack a kite for a birthday present but that she has no
money to buy one—even though the words "present," "money," or
any of their synonyms are not mentioned.[22]

These kinds of synthetic inference patterns are common in discourse, and their number and kind do not necessarily affect cohesion or comprehension, although their number and kind certainly
limit any attempt to formalize their relations. Commenting on col-
leagues' attempts to formalize multiple inference patterns, I. M.
Schlesinger poses the simple "John hit Mary," and asks:

> If John is a baby, it certainly does not follow that Mary is hurt, and if John
> is three, five, or seven years old the probability of her getting hurt
> increases correspondingly. Now, differences of probability are taken
> into account by Schank and Reiger, who make provisions for different
> "strengths" of inference. But the really serious problem, which they do
> not discuss, is the amount of information that has to be stored. They do
> mention that the "measure of the amount of injury done is a function of
> the hardness, heaviness, sharpness, etc. of the propelled object (with
> which one hits), and of the particular body part hit." But by granting this
> they conjure up a host of data, and one fails to see how they are going to
> cope with it.[23]

Inferences, Frames, and Cohesion

Besides its "simple" sentence-by-sentence application, inferencing also applies to whole passages. It is this role of inferences that
we now need to look at: the way they create "frames," "scripts,"
"paradigms," "semantic representations"—terms for the listener/
reader's equivalent to textual totality. Sentences and their implications are not comprehended in isolation, but as parts of wholes
which themselves are formed in part by reader inference. The

reader supplies inferences to determine the meaning of each individual sentence, and then to integrate that sentence with information she already knows. This integration produces a unifying context or situation into which further pieces of information may then be fit and understood. Thus a "dozen eggs, a loaf of bread, and tomato soup" make sense and exhibit cohesion when the reader constructs an appropriate frame for the information—a grocery list. As Rumelhart says, "The process of understanding a passage consists in finding a schema which will account for it."[24]

To illustrate the power, if not the necessity, of the schema or frame, we can look at an experiment done by Bransford and Johnson in which people were read the following passage, entitled "Watching a Peace March from the Fortieth Floor":

> The view was breathtaking. From the window one could see the crowd below. Everything looked extremely small from such a distance, but the colorful costumes could still be seen. Everyone seemed to be moving in one direction in an orderly fashion and there seemed to be little children as well as adults. The landing was gentle, and luckily the atmosphere was such that no special suits had to be worn. At first there was a great deal of activity. Later, when the speeches started, the crowd quieted down. The man with the television camera took many shots of the setting and the crowd. Everyone seemed glad when the music started.[25]

Given the context created by the title, most people were able to understand the passage until the sentence, "The landing was gentle, and luckily the atmosphere was such that no special suits had to be worn"; at that point their frame would not accommodate the new information. On the other hand, those given the same passage with the title, "A Space Trip to an Inhabited Planet," had no trouble with the landing sentence.

In this example, the reader constructs a temporary framework of interpretation which makes some meanings possible while excluding others. Each new piece of information reduces the possibilities until a quasi-deterministic structure, or comprehension context, emerges. This concept of the frame is straightforward and noncontroversial; its more impenetrable aspects emerge, however, when we ask the traditional structuralist question, "Where does the frame come from?" One school of research, the text-based school represented by Charniak, Hobbs, and Reiger, places the burden on the text to supply enough cues for a reader to invent a frame and "stresses the notion that the inference process looks for meaningful relationships between different propositions in the text."[26] In contrast, the model-based school of Lehnert, Rumelhart and Ortony, and Schank and Abelson presumes a priori structures that the reader brings to the text and that the text merely activates. This school

argues that a central purpose of inference is to synthesize an underlying model which organizes and augments the surface structure fragments in the text. In this view, inference is controlled by a target structure that specifies the *a priori* constraints on the kind of model to be synthesized. This target structure acts as an organizational principle for guiding a set of inference procedures.[27]

In light of language's dependence on world knowledge and in light of our own common sense experiences with language, the model-based approach seems intuitively to describe textual understanding best. In *Message Structure*, Rommetveit cites the situation of the middle-aged, married couple where "an interrogatory gaze from the wife in response to the visibly exposed gloomy tension of her husband at that moment may serve as a prelude to the—to the outsider—very cryptic remark 'Pot.' And the wife 'understands perfectly': what is worrying her husband at that particular moment is the possibility that their son Sam may start smoking pot."[28] Only the concept of an a priori frame composed either of a perfectly shared world view, as in this example, or of an imperfectly shared world view, as in texts, can explain language use.

Approaches to Frames

Even so, accepting the existence of frames and their a priori basis advances us only so far; given the "less than perfect synchronization of intentions and thought" between most people, the next question must be, What are the *textual* constituents of a frame?[29] Unfortunately, applied research in this area is minimal, although test-tube theories abound. Under the influence of recent linguistic advances, theoreticians have adapted transformational and case grammars'

distinction between deep and surface structure, as a means of dealing with the fact that people do not remember texts *verbatim*, and
thus as a means of resolving one of the cruxes involved in defining a
frame: "As for storage in memory, there is experimental evidence
that the sentence content or deep structure tended to be retained,
and surface form to be discarded."[30] Many theoreticians have relegated surface structure to the status of a nuisance, an irrelevancy
that has to be endured to get to the omnipotent deep structure:
"Phrase structure boundaries may thus serve as cues to deep structure relationships. Note, however, that the surface structure is not
accorded an independent status in the comprehension model."[31]
Such statements typify an almost wholesale bypassing of surface
structure by recent scholars, in favor of some form of deep structure. And while the components of the deep structure may vary according to particular theories—from propositions to cognitive structure to I-markers to nebulous nonlinguistic "meaning"—all these
theories share the same basic premise that single sentence deep-
structure analysis is the first step in the analysis of total discourse
structure. The informing correlative is always some variation of
transformational analysis. But this presumption, that the deep structure of a sentence, however defined, is analogous to the structure of
discourse, produces serious inconsistencies arising from a tenuous
initial hypothesis. Transformational grammar seeks to explain what
structures a sentence; discourse and comprehension analysis seek to
explain what structures a discourse; one predicates the sentence as
the unit of study, the other, the text. There is no reason in general
to assume that an answer to one set of questions will be transferable
to another set of questions; there is no reason in particular to assume that the transient, semantic/syntactic structures built during
sentence construction are similar to the larger structures of texts.
For instance, transformational grammars are verb-based, with parts
of sentences seen as instantiating verb frames. But in discourse
analysis one can easily imagine verbs being subordinated to nouns
or topics. Similarly, in their preoccupation with deep structure and
with semantics in general, these transformational theories do not
account for the fact that features such as articles, which for good reason are given low priority in sentence grammar, seem to be of con-
summate importance in discourse structure. In effect, comprehension theories modeled on transformational grammar assume

discourse to be one giant sentence made up of a list of ordered propositions, and thus provide neither analytic nor synthetic means for
going beyond simple sentence-by-sentence understanding to any
kind of larger, assimilative structure. Such theories do not really allow for the frame.

Even frankly granting the catch-all attractiveness of deep-
structure sentence analysis, and granting some correlation between
the deep structure of sentences and the total structure of discourse,
one feels that the preoccupation with deep structure has seriously
colored the few actual attempts to identify textual cues to comprehension. When faced with various possible conclusions from experiments, researchers today opt for deep structure. Kintsch, for
instance, arguing for propositional analysis, concludes that his propositions are "real units" because deep structure propositions, written as VA and VAO and representing sentences such as "The sentry
yawned" and "The travelers noticed a restaurant," were remembered as units by his subjects.[32] Then Ross Winterowd (1980) cites
Kintsch's study and says: "Fillmore (1968) explored the grammar of
propositions, and Kintsch (1974) demonstrated their psychological
reality."[33]

But one could just as easily conclude from Kintsch's findings that
his subjects remembered surface forms rather than deep structures,
because his propositional analysis is in fact congruent with traditional surface structure analysis. One feels that something already
congruent with an existing form requires more than a name change
to establish its separate existence, and that Kintsch is doing no more
than calling janitors "custodians."

On the other hand, researchers deliberately testing the reality of
surface forms have demonstrated that they affect reader comprehension in both positive and negative ways. As the division of a sentence
into its surface constituents is made more salient, so, too, is the sentence's comprehensibility increased. Trabasso found that sentence
subjects were identified faster in active sentences than in passive
sentences.[34] On the other hand, multiple embedded sentences, with
discontinuity of phrases, were found to impede comprehension.[35]

Given such evidence suggesting the integrity, even if not the Platonic reality, of surface forms, an analysis of their interactive effect
on comprehension and cohesion is very much in order. At the very
least, surface structure analysis can develop empirical data to help

refine our present models of discourse comprehension. Instead of viewing surface features as irrelevant nuisances, such analysis assumes that they represent an intermediate stage between sentence deep structure and discourse structure. In order to discern the structure and form of a house, one does not need to decompose its bricks into their elements; rather, one takes the bricks as given and tries to determine how their arrangement and order contribute to the house's stability and structure.

Textual Cues to Frames

As I suggested a few pages earlier, although deep structure theories of comprehension regularly fill the pages of journals and books, and although they claim to describe reader comprehension, few have exposed themselves to the hard reality of empirical testing. This final section will review the few reader-tested attempts to identify the textual constituents of a frame.

The most extensive investigation in this area is derived from Kintsch's propositional analysis. Kintsch and Janet Keenan, in "Reading Rate and Retention of the Number of Propositions," develop a concept of "superordinate" based on simple sequence.[36] Proposition A is superordinate to proposition B if (1) proposition A precedes proposition B, and (2) if both A and B share a common term. In recall tests based on this assumption, subjects were found consistently to recall superordinate propositions better than subordinate ones. The general applicability of this conception was confirmed by Waters, who tested third-grade, sixth-grade, and college students, all of whom recalled superordinate propositions better than subordinate ones.[37]

In Kintsch's memory model, this superordinate-subordinate relationship between propositions is not in itself equivalent to a text's frame, or "macrostructure," as he calls it; the relationship between propositions represents only one part of the macrostructure. The other set of relationships constituting the frame is that of proposition "importance." Gail McKoon, in "Organization of Information in Text Memory," used the following criterion for identifying "important" propositions: "So for the paragraphs used in the experiments, *intuition* determined the most important proposition."[38] Contributing to the researcher's intuition were: (1) surface structure cues, involving such devices as syntactic foregrounding and "surface order relations such as placing the topic sentence first"; and (2) "the relationship of the information in the text to the reader's knowledge of the world."[39] Combining this conception of importance with Kintsch's conception of superordinate, McKoon found that subjects best remembered propositions satisfying both criteria.

Two researchers, Bransford and Franks, have used a non-Kintschian conception of superordinate based explicitly on syntax. As precursors to sentence-combining, they conceive of "superordinate" as "wholistic semantic ideas," the nature of which are best understood by an example.[40] "The rock which rolled down the mountain crushed the tiny hut at the edge of the woods" represents the wholistic unit for the following individual sentences: "The rock rolled down the mountain"; "The rock crushed the hut"; "The hut was tiny"; "The hut was at the edge of the woods." Bransford and Franks found that subjects given such a series of four simple sentences did not identify as "new" any complex sentence containing three of the four simple sentences. However, when given a sentence incorporating only two of the simple sentences, subjects were less certain about whether or not the complex sentence was "new." Bransford and Franks interpret these results as a step toward defining the frame as a linguistic abstraction which exhausts semantic possibilities.

The final and most ambitious attempt to identify textual cues for a frame comes from Edward Crothers. In "Memory and the Recall of Discourse," Crothers tried to develop frames that incorporated both the implied rhetoric and the thematic content of a passage.[41] In his system, the rhetoric of a passage represented the superordinate node or frame, and was symbolized by logical connectives such as IS, WHY, OR, AND, and IF. These framing words were not stated in the text but inferred by Crothers. The actual content of the passage, and the words or concepts representing that content, were treated as subordinate subtrees to these superordinate connectives. Within this classification, Crothers' expectations that superordinates would be recalled more often than subordinates was not confirmed; nor was the corollary hypothesis confirmed, that secondary subtrees would be recalled less often than primary subtrees. Thus Crothers' equation of the frame with the implied and abstracted rhetoric of a passage was not confirmed.

In discussing his negative results, Crothers concedes that factors not measured by his system, particularly item repetition, probably contribute to a reader's apprehension of a frame. Thematization, or the establishment of a referent through associated noun phrases, has in fact been shown to contribute to the reader's sense of totality. Charles Perfetti and Susan Goldman tested subjects for their recall of thematized referents as against nonthematized referents. They note that in their experiment it is not simply a word that is thematized by a referent: a passage that identifies Dr. Jones and "relates that he is a surgeon, is thematizing a referent that is realized by the expressions Dr. Jones, the surgeon, the doctor, he and other noun phrases identifying the referent."[42] Under these circumstances, the thematized referent became a more reliable recall cue than nonthematized referents.

In retrospect, we can see that the shared constant in these experiments is term repetition. Although only Perfetti and Goldman in their thematization study explicitly tested the effect of repetition, item recurrence contributed to the success of Kintsch's work, to that of his disciples, and to that of Bransford and Franks, whereas the failure of Crothers' taxonomy to provide for item recurrence probably explains his negative results. Even though the experiments ostensibly tested term order and synthesis, the obvious prerequisite to such measurement is the actual presence of a repeated term(s). Limited as these results are, they confirm the hypothesis in chapter 2 that cohesion consists primarily of unity, the presence of a repeated term.

Furthermore, these experiments, and others cited throughout the chapter, confirm the hypothesis that unity dominates coherence. A minimum and necessary threshold of cohesion is attained through the unity created by the repeated term, so that comprehension can be impeded but never fully blocked by "bad" or inappropriate order.

Because of the theoretical assumptions underlying these experiments, only one kind of order was tested, the basic chainlike transitivity established by sequences in the form A is B, B is C, and so on—or what Frase in his experiment labeled "good order." The results of the experiments indicate that such an order clearly does exist, and does aid in comprehension and cohesion. In an independent textual study, Daneš labeled the order as "simple linear progression," in which the rheme of one sentence (basically the sentence's predicate) becomes the theme (subject) of the next. However, he also identified three other common recurrence patterns:

1. passages with run-through themes (a sequence of sentences with the same theme but different rheme);
2. progression of derived theme;
3. development of a split-rheme (the themes of successive sentences are co-members of a concept forming the rheme of the initial sentence).[43]

Not only do such additional patterns of item recurrence exist, but the actual contribution to cohesion of the A is B order must be qualified. Of the following sentence sequences, only the first one is cohesive:

Roberto Clemente was the greatest Pirate rightfielder of all times. The Pirates have been trying to replace him with Dave Parker, but unsuccessfully.

I don't like you. You are a breadboard. Breadboards are made of wood. Wood is grown in forests.

As the sequences illustrate, at least part of the cohesive power of the A is B order derives from the semantic relations of the item recurrences themselves. Thus the explanation for any success in the cited experiments must be modified: if some semantic compatibility or logic already exists between recurring items, the A is B order will then facilitate cohesion. This necessary modification supports the hypothesis in chapter 1 that while cohesion consists of both unity and coherence, unity dominates coherence, and coherence is a function of unity.

Finally, even though all the experiments tested only the A is B, B is C order, different researchers, working with different texts, were consistently able to abstract recurrence patterns—the core of cohesion—so that the hypothesis in chapter 2 that cohesion patterns manifest structural as well as semantic totalities is not only confirmed, but partially instantiated.

Beginning with the analytic overlay provided by Bühler's field theory of shared cultures, conventions, and language, this chapter first explored the role of inferences in line-by-line sentence comprehension, focusing only on recurrence chains with fairly simple set-relations, and posited an ease-of-inference measure based on the Aristotelian enthymeme. It also explored the role of inferences in passage comprehension, suggesting some of the textual cues that guide a reader's comprehension schema.

As a concluding reflection on the psycholinguistic work reviewed in this chapter, one must feel simultaneously a meagerness and a plentitude: a plentitude because the review obviously selected only the most germane articles from literally hundreds; a meagerness because the articles tend merely to confirm one's intuitive ideas about reader comprehension. (One suspects that this meagerness itself contributes to the profusion of comprehension theories.) I think one must also feel a certain self-irony about attempts to formalize the tremendous and analogic capacities of the human mind in one of its most subjective and personal experiences:

> A text is timeless, universal, objective, speaks to anyone who is literate, and reveals to him a self-contained meaning. Yet this objective and universal character can be realized only through the subjectivity of some reader; thus the burden of interpretation. Though a text is always about a world or a possible world, it does not refer to a world outside itself, for its world is created in the dialectic between itself and the reader.[44]

4

Single Term Paragraphs

AS THE PREVIOUS TWO CHAPTERS HAVE INDICATED, THERE IS both experimental evidence and theoretical motivation for positing the existence of some underlying structure for discourse units. Viewed as a property of the text, the underlying structure represents a norm similar to Jonathan Culler's totalities; as a characteristic of readers and the reading process, it represents an integrating and interpretive strategy similar to the psychologists's frames. Implicit in both these perspectives is the notion of form, "the principle of unity which determines the nature of a concrete whole . . . which does not arise out of the mere combination of parts; it is rather that prior principle which imposed on them determines their relationships."[1] The principles of any such ontological model depend, of course, on the level and scope of the discourse units considered, whether the traditional domain of literary critics debating spatial forms in novels, or the domain of discourse analysts seeking the frames or macrostructures of children's stories. The aim of this chapter is to look at a less abstract and perhaps more primary level of form: the organization and integration of sentences into paragraphs.

If, as Ross Winterowd remarked, cohesion is virtually synonymous with form, then the markers for cohesion at the paragraph level should lead to a description of paragraph form. Indeed, the paragraph, by virtue of its traditional definition as a discourse unit that develops a single idea, offers itself as a logical choice for exploring, testing, and articulating the concept of an informing totality. As a formal structure, the English paragraph received little attention until 1877, when Alexander Bain included a forty-five page chapter on the paragraph in his *English Composition and Rhetoric*. Although rhetoricians in his own time largely ignored Bain's work, later rhetoric and composition books canonized his definition and description of the paragraph. Bain's forty-five pages shaped a view of the paragraph that has lasted essentially unchanged for a hundred years.

As Bain defined it, the paragraph is "a collection of sentences with unity of purpose . . . that handles and exhausts a complete topic." [2] Among his six paragraph rules, the third recommended that the opening sentence "indicate with prominence the subject of the paragraph," thus giving rise to the concept of the topic sentence. Over the years, Bain's definition has become synonymous with the textbooks' paragraph and the staple of composition and rhetoric courses; "later rhetoricians tinkered with the language of this [Bain's] definition, but without improving upon or substantially changing the original insight." [3]

Yet like the concept of the totality or the frame, the concepts of the paragraph and the topic sentence, so intuitively obvious, defy unambiguous definition. What constitutes unity of purpose? What constitutes a complete idea? The most basic insights are also the most resistant to definition. One finds paragraphs with apparently more than one main idea, paragraphs with implied main ideas, multiple paragraphs that can be collapsed into one, paragraphs of one sentence and paragraphs of pages. Faced with this onslaught of qualifications and appendages, rhetoricians have begun to question, if not reject, the paragraph as a viable unit:

> Since every paragraph of the essay is part of the general flow, it is difficult to find in many paragraphs anything so static that it can be isolated as the single idea, or topic, of that paragraph. The notion that every paragraph must have a topic sentence is hence misleading. [4]

> [The paragraph] is simply a convenient grouping of sentences. In a progression of sentences a few places will be more suited to indentation than others, but you can justify indentations before almost any sentence of sophisticated prose. [5]

Reporting on an informal experiment in "When Is A Paragraph?", Arthur Stern describes the results when he asked his students to divide an excerpt from Brooks and Warren's *Fundamentals of Good Writing*. The results were erratic: "Some students divided the passage into two paragraphs, others into three, still others into four or five . . . only five students out of more than 100 who have tried the experiment have paragraphed the passage precisely as Brooks and Warren originally did."[6]

Confirming these results were the findings of a research project by Richard Braddock, "Frequency and Placement of Topic Sentences in Expository Prose." Braddock examined a corpus of 25 essays published in magazines like the *Atlantic Monthly*, *Harper's*, and the *New Yorker* for four kinds of topic sentences: the simple direct statement; the delayed completion, in which the topic sentence is initiated by one T-unit but completed by another; the assembled topic sentence, in which the topic sentence is built from phrases and clauses through the text; and finally, the inferred topic sentence, in which the topic sentence is implied even though it cannot be directly assembled from the original passage. Braddock concluded: "It is just not true that most expository paragraphs have topic sentences in that (simple direct) sense. Even when simple and delayed-completion topic sentences are combined into the category 'explicit topic sentences' . . . the frequency reaches only 55% of all entries."[7]

Yet counterbalancing Braddock's result is the positive one obtained by Frank Koen, Alton Becker, and Richard Young. In a study similar to Stern's but much more rigorously executed, they asked students to paragraph uninterrupted texts. They concluded from the results that, "It is apparent that the S's (subjects) agree with each other in their judgements of paragraphing boundaries in both English and nonsense passages. Paragraphing, then, is a reliable phenomenon."[8]

Given these conflicting results, most current researchers have stopped looking for a Platonic paragraph, and instead seek to identify and describe different kinds of actual paragraphs. The remainder of this chapter, in the spirit of the great Francis Christensen's call for different kinds of "yardsticks" to measure different kinds of paragraphs, analyzes one relatively simple kind—the series united by a single common term—but a kind which also represents one of Jonathan Culler's rudimentary totalities.[9]

The Series United by a Common Term

The series manifests the simplest form of intransitive-stative cohesion, attainable through the most rudimentary kind of unity, and it is also the simplest paragraph structure. It is created by a sequence of sentences sharing a single term so as to establish a continuous chain of antecedents and referents. The following example is patently dull and boorish:

> The Char-Bar is a bar on High Street. The Char-Bar swings. It permits dancing. The bar specializes in foreign beers. The Char-Bar attracts weirdos. It seats 198 people.

But it fulfills the basic requirements of unity—term dominance—and hence cohesion, and in fact constitutes the basic structural paradigm for many more sophisticated paragraphs.

Dominance is attained not simply by the presence of the term "Char-Bar" or its pronoun substitutes in each sentence, but by these items' appearing consistently in the subject position. If a term is repeated in each sentence but does not appear in the subject position, dominance is not attained, and the sequence is not cohesive:

> Alfred likes peaches. Oregon doesn't grow peaches. Peaches contain nitrogen. We have a peach tree in our backyard. No one throws rotten peaches at politicians or ball players. Cut five peaches and sprinkle with sugar. Do you think peach melba would be a good dessert?

Once the repeated term "peaches" appears in the predicate position, it forfeits the inherently limiting power of the subject position and is itself "subjected" to at least five other topics: Alfred, Oregon, we, no one, you. As these two samples indicate, cohesion requires the meshing of both semantic and syntactic information and, at least for some paragraph types, is not primarily a semantic phenomenon as Halliday and Hasan claim, and can be defined operationally.[10]

As noted in chapter 2, psychologists have shown that semantic dominance is achieved most readily through item repetition that establishes an equivalence chain; they also reported that the syntactic position of the repeated items directly affects readers' perception of dominance: thematized items appearing in the subject position are better remembered than thematized items in the object position, which merely reminds us that English is a language of synthesis and position dependent on syntactic information. In typical simple sentences the most important syntactic position is the subject position. In the first sample, the appearance of "Char-Bar" in each sentence produced a thematized item and semantic dominance; its recurrences specifically in the subject position then give it syntactic dominance as well, and this convergence of semantic and syntactic dominance in individual sentences makes "Char-Bar" the dominant term of the paragraph. Thus, (1) when a term attains semantic dominance through repetition or equivalence, and (2) when the term appears consistently in the subject or dominant noun phrase position, we have the simple but necessary paradigm for the single-term paragraph. The sheer repetition of a single term creates semantic consistency, and the consistent appearance of the term in the subject (or dominant noun phrase) slot thematizes it syntactically.

This account of cohesion as the convergence of semantics with syntax is also an account of paragraph form. Only when the repeated term keeps appearing in the subject position does the repetition create the rudimentary unified structure that Kenneth Burke and Jonathan Culler independently identify as the series united by a common term.

Obviously not all paragraphs read as crudely and disjointedly as the Char-Bar text. The next few pages will examine variations of the basic pattern, paragraphs that move beyond the minimal requirements into more complex and interesting manifestations of the paradigm structure.

At this stage, we can look at a paragraph in which the dominant term is not literally repeated but is inferrable from the text. The use of ellipsis, which in turn requires the reader to make inferences, is very common to descriptive paragraphs such as the following by Truman Capote:

The truck was of the Ford pick-up type. Its interior smelled strongly of sun warmed leather and gasoline. The broken speedometer registered a petrified twenty. Rainstreaks and crushed insects blurred the windshield of which one section was shattered in a bursting star pattern. A toy skull ornamented the gear shift. The wheels bump-bumped over the rising, dipping, curving Paradise Chapel Highway.[11]

Written without discourse ellipsis, the passage would read something like this:

> The truck was of the Ford pick-up type. The truck had an interior. The interior smelled strongly of gasoline. The truck had a speedometer. The broken speedometer registered a petrified twenty. The truck had a windshield. Rainstreaks and crushed insects blurred the windshield of which one section was shattered in a bursting star pattern. The truck had a gear shift. A toy skull ornamented the gear shift. The truck had wheels. The wheels bump-bumped over the rising, dipping, curving Paradise Chapel Highway.

Even in the expanded text, no single term appears in every sentence, although "truck" makes a strong bid for attention by its presence in six of the eleven sentences. The absence of a repeated term immediately weakens the basic paradigm: if no term appears in every sentence, the term repeated most often becomes the basis for the equivalence chain. While such a qualification may have to be invoked eventually, it is not our only recourse with this example, because a transformational analysis in fact provides every sentence with the recurring term "truck." If we assume that definite articles are reduced possessives, then we can reconstruct sentences such as: "The truck's interior smelled strongly of sun warmed leather and gasoline," "The truck's speedometer registered a petrified twenty," and so on. This reconstruction is consistent with the first expanded version since the same bridging assumptions are posited, but in this instance they are presumed to be parts of sentences instead of individual sentences.

Having established a repeated term in each sentence, we need to determine the degree of agreement or concord between that semantically important term and its syntactic prominence. Continuing with a transformational analysis of the sentences, we have no trouble: the bridging assumption is in the highest, hence dominating, sentence node. Thus the sentences, "Rainstreaks and crushed insects blurred the windshield, of which one section was shattered in a bursting star pattern," and "A toy skull ornamented the gear shift"—where the implied "truck" is in the object position—nevertheless exhibit concord between the repeated term in the deep structure (although not in the surface structure) and the syntactically dominant position.

Happily, Capote did not write my reconstructed version. If he had, the result would have been another ponderous Char-Bar paragraph. Instead he wrote a self-sufficient but abbreviated version of the deep structure version, reminding us that all discourse is elliptical. What Capote also did was to maintain the delicate and dynamic balance between suggestive repetition—the core of unity and cohesion—and boring repetition. He transformed the paragraph from a skeletal paradigm to an artful text.

Neither in the Capote paragraph nor in the Char-Bar paragraph did any of the intermediate sentences contain direct links with their immediate predecessors. Capote's well-wrought, unified and quite elegant paragraph nevertheless did not lock each sentence into position through some immediate repetition or transition word; indeed, individual sentences could easily be reordered. This possibility contradicts the admonition in composition textbooks that, in well-wrought paragraphs, individual sentences must be locked in place. It also contradicts Halliday and Hasan's global prediction that sentence links—repetitions, basically—will cluster at the paragraph's center, so that the number of links can be graphically represented as follows:

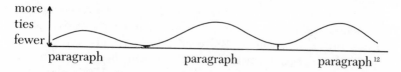

more
ties
fewer

paragraph   paragraph   paragraph [12]

Instead, Capote's paragraph fulfills Lathrop's prediction that unity of connection emerges from and is shaped by the total structure. Cohesion is a general effect for which there is no simple prescription. Different kinds of textual totalities will have different cohesion patterns, and, as Christensen said, we need different yardsticks for identifying these patterns, which also involve different kinds of paragraph structures.

Both the preceding examples were paragraphs of description, but the paradigm of a series united by a common term can also describe paragraphs traditionally labeled as paragraphs of example, which suggests that we are dealing with a fundamental method for classifying paragraph structures. The following paragraph of exemplification also manifests the single-term pattern:

Admen and packagers, of course, are not the only euphemizers. Almost any way of earning a salary above the level of ditchdigging is known as a profession rather than a job. Janitors for several years have been elevated by image conscious unions to the status of "custodians"; nowadays, a teen-rock guitarist with three chords to his credit can class himself with Horowitz as a "recording artist." Cadillac dealers refer to autos as "pre-owned" rather than "secondhand." Government researchers concerned with old people call them "senior citziens." Ads for credit and department stores refer to "convenient terms"—meaning 18% annual interest payable at the convenience of the creditor.[13]

Here, as in the Capote paragraph, the repeated term is implied rather than stated. Through some back reconstruction, we can identify it as some form of "euphemizers." Every reader, I think, will agree that sentences two through six give examples or instances of the generalization in sentence one, based on the dictionary definition of "euphemizers," and she will mentally insert "for example" or "for instance" before each of those sentences. Such terms as "for instance" or "for example" are transition words which operate as whole sentence modifiers; transformationally, they are members of the sentence's highest syntactic constituent, just as possessives were in the preceding example. However, if there is to be concord between the highest syntactical constituent and the repeated term, the repeated term must occupy that constituent. The implied "for example" or "for instance" presently occupying that slot are not "euphemizers." Thus the bridging assumption that first suggested a simple "for example" must now be reexamined. "For example" is not a complete assertion; that is, it is not a complete predication or argument, so that we must presume it to be a condensed form of the complete bridging assumption. To make our analysis reflect our intuitive understanding of the text, we need a complete bridging assumption that answers the question, "Example of what?", with "that there are other euphemizers." This complete bridging assumption (or some version of it) prefixes and provides context for sentences two through six, in which "for example" or "for instance" are condensed placeholders for the bridging assumption. (Instead of viewing "for example" or "for instance" as elliptical phrases, we might also view them as discourse substitutes comparable to "one" in sentence analysis.) Sentence two, in which no example of euphemizers is named, requires an additional inferencing step; the reader must supply "society," or "people in general," to go with the unions, guitarist, Cadillac dealers, and government researchers named in the other sentences. While the actual bridging assumptions used by different readers may vary, and while the actual steps taken in tracking "for example" to "euphemizers" may still be debatable, nevertheless each reader's reconstruction will always lead back to "euphemizers." This suggests that although textbooks would classify the euphemizer paragraph as exemplification rather than description, it is in fact another version of the series united by a common term.

Variations in Position of the Dominant Term

In the preceding analysis, no acknowledgement was made that "euphemizers" first occurs in the predicate position, whereas in the earlier samples the repeated term consistently appeared in the subject and/or highest syntactical position. In the euphemizer paragraph, the repeated term first appears in the predicate position and then consistently in the highest syntactical position. This is not an ad hoc exception but simply a refinement of the concept of syntactic dominance as the concord between a repeated term's location and the sentence's syntactically highest constituent. As the peaches nontext demonstrated, in a single-term sentence sequence where the sentences' subjects and predicates are respectively in the highest noun phrase and verb phrase slots, the repeated term cannot consistently appear in the predicate position because it forfeits its limiting power of sentence subject. However, since a sentence's subject and predicate are syntactically coequal, the euphemizer paragraph does not violate but refines our definition of dominance.

We should remember that the first sentence in any text does not predict what will follow; our sense of pattern or structure develops as we proceed through the text. We could have encountered a sequence like the following:

Admen and packagers are not the only euphemizers. But they are
the most influential and ubiquitous. They attack our senses and
form our opinions about "products" that once were not products,
like presidential candidates.

Barthes describes our assembly process thus:

> Whoever reads a text collects bits of information under the generic
> names of actions (Walk, Assassination, Rendez-vous), and it is this name
> which creates the sequence. The sequence comes to exist only at the mo-
> ment when and because one can name it; it develops according to the
> rhythm of this naming process, which seeks and confirms.[14]

Certainly some paragraphs exhibit inconsistent placement of the
repeated term as it shifts between the subject and predicate positions. The degree to which readers might find such paragraphs cohesive is ultimately a function of quantity: the more often the repeated term appears in the subject position, the more likely the
passage will be perceived as cohesive. Presumably a statistical study
of shifts in position would yield a set of formulas: a paragraph of five
sentences requires the repeated term to occupy the subject position
three times, and so on. Such a study would presumably measure the
skew from the paradigm and help distinguish borderline cases of
cohesion.

A second argument for viewing the predicate initial position as
simply a refinement of the basic paradigm is based on the sentence's
discourse function. Discourse involves thematic progression (although the samples thus far examined are not primarily characterized by their transitivity) and progression is attained by the conjoining of arguments. At the sentence level, the grammatical functions
of subject and predicate accomplish this progression when the subject is understood as what is being talked about and the predicate
as what is being said about the subject. Discourse analysts have developed various terminologies for this progression: theme/rheme;
known/unknown; given/new. Despite the different terminologies,
each schema seeks to capture a sentence's message structure as it
progresses from the given, the known, the understood, to the new
and the unknown. John Erskine describes this fundamental characteristic of communication this way:

What you wish to say is found not in the noun but in what you add to qualify the noun. The noun is only a grappling iron to hitch your mind to the reader's. The noun by itself adds nothing to the reader's information; it is the name of something he knows already, and if he does not know it, you cannot do business with him.[15]

Yet just as sentences move from the known to the unknown, the unknown becomes known and shared, and a new progression is initiated. The particular sequence of $Subject_1/Predicate_1$ to

$$\left\{ \begin{array}{l} Subject_2 \\ Predicate_1 \end{array} \right\} /Predicate_2,$$

or $A:B$; $B:C$, is the ideal schema for this movement. It duplicates Frase's documented conception of "good order," and rhetorically it conforms with the basic information psychology of introducing the unknown through the known. As we shall see shortly, this particular shift from subject to predicate to subject is one of the most common forms of paragraph juncture for the series united by a common term. Besides opening paragraphs, this sequence just as frequently closes them, and in both cases provides content connections with adjacent paragraphs.

Intrasentential Links Within the Series

Thus far the sample paragraphs exhibiting the series united by the common term have not been characterized by the usual devices of coherence, namely, direct links between sentences; in each sample, sentences could be moved without affecting the reader's sense of cohesion. This structure does not, however, prohibit immediate links between sentences, as suggested by the following example, which probably represents the most structurally interesting and complex variation of the common-term paradigm. We return to euphemisms:

From a Greek word meaning "to use words of good omen," "euphemism" is the substitution of a pleasant term for a blunt one—telling it like it isn't. Euphemism has probably existed since the beginning of language. As long as there have been things of which man thought the less said the better, there have been better ways of saying less. In everyday conversation, the euphemism is, at worst, a necessary evil; at its best, it is a handy verbal tool to avoid making enemies needlessly, or shocking friends. Language purists and the blunt spoken may wince when a young woman at a party coyly asks for directions to the "powder room," but to most people this kind of familiar euphemism is probably no more harmful or annoying than, say, the split infinitive.[16]

In this paragraph, we have something a bit more satisfying to most readers than the earlier samples; instead of a text in which the bare bones of the structure rattle about for our attention, we find the structure fleshed out, more robust but also less conspicuous. Even a cursory examination reveals a repeated term—"euphemism"—in each sentence, although sentence three substitutes a phrase synonym, "better ways of saying less." "Euphemism" occupies the subject slot in each sentence except sentence three, which again has the empty "there" in the subject position.

Two qualities distinguish this paragraph from its predecessors: it conveys more information through more complex and heavily modified sentences, and it uses that additional information to link each sentence to its immediate neighbor. These sentences cannot be moved around as easily as in the earlier examples, if, indeed, they can be moved at all.

Chapter 2 predicted increased coherence through more complex sentence constructions, so that will not be elaborated on here. Instead, we will look at the form and effect of the immediate sentence links. In any of the earlier paragraphs, the authors could have chosen to head each sentence with an enumeration transition word such as "first," "second," "next," and so on. One has little reason and less desire to believe that such insertions would have enhanced the paragraphs. They would have been superfluous to reader comprehension, and with their wide applicability convey little information in themselves. They would have been perceived as mechanical vestiges of a Freshman English lesson. But in the euphemism example, the traditional transition words before individual sentences (with the exception of "for example" or "for instance" before the last sentence) would be semantically incongruous and downright illogical. Here the immediate sentence links are attained through message-contributing adverbials, such as "since the beginning of time," "as long as," " in everyday conversation," "at worst," and "at best." Besides conveying new information, these adverbials lock individual sentences in place and create mini-contexts for adjacent sentences within the larger series pattern—even though the adverbials themselves do not enter directly into the main series pattern of "euphemism." Barthes observed this phenomenon in larger discourse units, labeling the two patterns, "satellites" and "kernels." He distinguished "between 'kernels' which link up with one another to form plot and 'catalysts' or 'satellites' which are attached to kernels but do not themselves establish sequences."[17]

Skews from the Paradigm

Finally we must consider the validity of the preceding concepts by applying them as a standard by which to evaluate paragraphs which are not fully cohesive but which are nevertheless comprehensible.

As a test paragraph we can consider the following by Scott Momaday, a paragraph that may seem attractive on first reading because of its descriptive and allusive qualities, but which leaves us finally with a sense of looseness and unraveling, of weak cohesion:

[1] A single knoll rises out of the plain in Oklahoma, north and west of the Wichita Range. [2] For my people, the Kiowas, it is an old landmark, and they give it the name of Rainy Mountain. [3] The hardest weather in the world is there. [4] Winter brings blizzards, hot tornadic winds arise in the spring, and in summer the prairie is an anvil's edge. [5] The grass turns brittle and brown, and it cracks beneath your feet. [6] There are green belts along the rivers and creeks, linear groves of hickory and pecan, willow and witch hazel. [7] At a distance in July or August the steaming foliage seems almost to writhe in fire. [8] Great green and yellow grasshoppers are everywhere in the tall grass, popping up like corn to sting the flesh, and tortoises crawl about on the red earth, going nowhere in plenty of time. [9] Loneliness is an aspect of the land. [10] All things in the plain are isolate; there is no confusion of objects in the eye, but *one* hill or *one* tree or *one* man. [11] To look upon that landscape in the early morning, with the sun at your back, is to lose the sense of proportion. [12] Your imagination comes to life, and this, you think, is where Creation was begun.[18]

The paragraph opens with a sputter and indecision, as the first candidate for dominant term, "knoll," appears first as subject, again as subject, and then as predicate, meanwhile vying for dominance with "Kiowas," which appears first in a superordinate position and then in the subject position of the compound sentence two. Sentence three partially resolves this confusion with its anaphoric "there," which at first is inferred as a reference to "knoll." That inference is sustained until the appearance of "prairie" in sentence four, which requires inferential retracking either to "plain" in sentence one, or to some general concept such as locale, which will include both the knoll and the plain.

Sentences five through eight run the reader through another disconcerting string of inferences: the "grass" of sentence five is apparently the prairie's grass; sentence six implies that the prairie also has rivers and trees, an ecological and therefore semantic incongruity; sentence eight's bridging assumption returns the reader to the "grass" of sentence five—violating the ordering principle for inferences developed in chapter 3—and then requires a further bridging assumption, that "the prairie has red earth." By now we have a disparate collection rather than a consistent series of bridging assumptions: the prairie has grass, a defining characteristic of prairies; the prairie also has trees and rivers and creeks, an apparently anomalous feature of this particular prairie; and the prairie has red earth, a differentiating but not anomalous characteristic of this particular prairie. These bridging assumptions contrast sharply with those in the Capote and euphemism paragraphs, which were not only consistent with one another but also manifested a second set of relations by means of that consistency: parts of a truck and types of euphemizers. Consistency in the bridging assumptions seems a very conspicuous feature, if not a requirement in strongly cohesive repeated-term paragraphs. One can contrast bridging assumptions in the Momaday paragraph with those in the following Barbara Tuchman paragraph, which consistently refer to "effects of the plague":

The plague raged at terrifying speed, increasing the impression of horror. In a given locality it accomplished its kill within four to six months except in the larger cities, where it struck again in the spring after lying dormant in winter. The death rate in Avignon was said to have claimed half the population, of whom ten thousand were buried in the first six

weeks in a massive grave. The mortality was in fact erratic. Some com-
munities whose last survivors fled in despair were simply wiped out and
disappeared from the map forever, leaving only a grassed-over hump as
their mortal trace.[19]

Here is a clear sequence of bridging assumptions—the death
rate, the mortality, the survivors who fled—whose very constancy
enhances the paragraph's cohesion.

The other inconsistency in the Momaday text—the failure of the
repeated term to appear regularly in the superordinate syntactic
position—involves what is probably the most important single vari-
able for determining the relative cohesiveness of single-term paragraphs in which the repeated term is explicit rather than implicit.
Here is another example, on weasel words:

A weasel word is "a word used in order to evade or retreat from a direct
or forthright statement or position." (Webster) In other words, if we can't
say it, we'll weasel it. And, in fact, a weasel word has become more than
just an evasion or retreat. We've trained our weasels. They can do anything. They can make you hear things that aren't being said, accept as
truths things that have only been implied and believe things that have
only been suggested. Come to think of it, not only do we have our
weasels trained, but they, in turn, have got you trained. When *you* hear
a weasel word, you automatically hear the implication. Not the real
meaning, but the meaning *it* wants *you* to hear. So if you're ready for a
little re-education, let's take a good look under a strong light at the two
kinds of weasel words.[20]

Even though "weasel word" (or "weasel") is a repeated term in all
the sentences, it never quite attains dominance because of the competition for subject position from "we" and "you" in the various sentences. A less obvious competitor is the author, who inserts himself
through the transition phrases, "in fact" and "come to think of it."
These transitions fall into the category of attitudinal disjuncts, common devices for authorial intervention. "In fact" and "come to think
of it" dominate two out of ten sentences, in which the author places
a self-highlighting phrase in the highest syntactic position and thus
keeps "weasel word" from fulfilling the second criterion for term

dominance: appearing in the subject position and/or highest syntactic position.

Ramifications of the Series Paradigm

The shifting and intermingling of terms in sentences' highest syntactic slots ultimately affects the reader's sense of paragraph juncture, or closure, a concept vital to any overall view of paragraph structure. Where and how does a paragraph conclude? Some pages ago I suggested that shifting a repeated term from the subject position to the predicate position, and vice versa, frequently signals closure for this kind of paragraph structure. In the weasel word paragraph, as just noted, the author's mishandling of this shift contributed to the paragraph's weak cohesion. But it is important nevertheless to recognize the power of this pattern, even when it is used medially rather than terminally; regardless of the length of its development, that is, the number of actual sentences involved before the shift from subject to predicate position occurs, a unit is still created:

> We've trained our weasels. They can do anything. They can make you hear things that aren't being said, accept as truths things that have only been implied, and believe things that have only been suggested.

Indeed, because of its power either to introduce or develop a term, this pattern enables one to predict paragraph junctures in single-term paragraphs. Given the following paragraph, readers would either recognize a whole unit or else see junctures at "In so far as we are . . ." or at "This is the essence of rational behavior":

> A sign is anything that announces the existence or the imminence of some event, the presence of a thing or a person, or a change in the state of affairs. There are signs of the weather, signs of danger, signs of future good or evil, signs of what the past has been. In every case a sign is closely bound up with something to be noted or expected in experience. It is always part of the situation to which it refers, though the reference may be remote in time and space. In so far as we are led to note or expect the signified event we are making correct use of a sign. This is the es-

sence of rational behavior, which animals show in varying degrees. It is entirely realistic, being closely bound up with the actual objective course of history—learned by experience, and cashed in or voided by future experience.[21]

Just as the first sentences define a sign, with congruent placement of the term "sign" in the subject position, the latter sentences signal a new perspective and appropriately move predicate material to the subject position; in both instances, syntax instantiates structure and rhetoric.

Furthermore, because this pattern of the series united by a common term can be instantiated through any number of sentences, it defines not only complete paragraphs, but also subunits of more complex, double- and triple-term paragraphs, as in the following example containing a subunit on "cheap cases":

It is commonly believed that a reader's interest is attracted by a case with which he can identify himself—there but for the grace of God, et cetera. But if the average tabloid reader were murdered, his misfortune would not receive much coverage in the average tabloid. He would be a "cheap case." Essentially, a cheap case involves what tabloid editors consider to be cheap people. This includes all working-class people, such as factory hands, waitresses and the unemployed. It also includes farmers, usually brushed aside as "hillbilly stuff." Alcoholics, whose antics are sometimes extremely entertaining, come under the same ban. So do Negroes, Mexicans, Puerto Ricans and other "lesser breeds without law." This causes some difficulty for the wire services since the current fashion is to delete any references to a criminal's race as "irrelevant." Thus an editor who might begin by showing great interest in a murder would cut the story down to a few paragraphs after learning that it involved a "Jig," but he would not publicly divulge the dread word that motivated his editing— and, of course, his editorial columns would continue to clamor for civil rights.[22]

As the next chapter will argue, the series united by a common term seems to be one of the most basic structural parts of paragraphs, and it presents a means by which to begin analyzing the hierarchy of structures in an entire text. Indeed, this pattern exemplifies one characteristic of Barthes' satellites and kernels, namely, that the satellites attach themselves to the kernels but do not themselves form a sequence. While sentence modifiers are the satellites in single-term paragraphs, the basic kernel pattern of the series united by a common term becomes the satellite in more complex paragraphs, as in the preceding example. As Culler describes it: "Kernel and satellite are purely relational terms: what is a kernel at one level of plot structure will become a satellite at another, and a sequence of kernels may itself be taken up by a thematic unit."[23]

Another issue to be addressed in the next chapter is the topic sentence. In the present chapter, a whole happy family of well-adjusted paragraphs shared not a single topic sentence among them. All had topics—the repeated term—but none had a topic sentence. The euphemizer paragraph's opening line, "Admen and packagers are not the only euphemizers," was the only possible candidate. Unlike the other opening sentences, this one contains some conjoined argument: "not the only euphemizers." However, because the conjoinment involves adverb, adjective, and noun, it does not create a topic sentence of noun plus predicate. One can substitute "Parents and teachers are not the only euphemizers" in the first sentence, retain all the other sentences, and still maintain the paragraph's cohesion. What the euphemizer paragraph does have is a more refined topic than the other paragraphs.

That paragraphs exist without topic sentences has been widely observed. This chapter extends that observation to suggest that the appropriateness of using a topic sentence depends on the paragraph's particular structure as a totality. If one assumes that a topic sentence requires the support and development of an argument made up of at least a noun plus a predicate, then the textual manifestation of that development would require at least two recurrence chains, and we would thus be dealing with a different kind of structure from the single-term totality.

If one carries the issue of the topic sentence one step further and asks: Should paragraphs exist without topic sentences? the foregoing analysis in this chapter suggests, quite simply, that it all depends. It depends on the kind of paragraph structure. The series united by a common term excludes the topic sentence by definition, and the paragraphs examined here have all been comprehensible, even stylish and elegant, without the aid of a topic sentence.

On the assumption that cohesion defines relations and that relations define structure, this chapter has developed the concept of paragraph structure. What can be said about the nature of this structure? First, structure may well be too powerful a concept when applied to discourse, if one means by it something like atomic structure where all elements are interdependent and any change or addition produces a new totality, a new chemical. On the other hand, if one interprets structure as a pattern whose certain minimal requirements must be met, then the concept seems appropriate and is analogous to the "structure" of an alphabet letter, a circle, or a box, whose defining patterns must be established but whose size is not consequential.

Paragraph size, or more accurately length, and eventually paragraph closure, seem to be the limiting conditions for any attempt to describe paragraph structure. There is obviously some truth to the claim that people paragraph at whim. Paragraph structures are also obviously affected by physical and genre conventions. Newspaper paragraphs differ in length from textbook paragraphs, letter paragraphs from typed paragraphs, and so on. However, the methodology outlined in this chapter, along with the concept of kernels and satellites, seems to provide a means to predict where an author will *not* paragraph. If one assumes paragraphs to have *some* basic structure, any paragraphing that obscures or contradicts that structure would be perceived as lacking cohesion. In this respect, my analysis and methodology may be seen to extend previous paragraph research. Becker and Christensen, the modern pioneers in this area, based their analyses primarily on rhetorical relations: topic, comment, restriction; coordination and subordination.[24]

Just as those relations describe paragraph characteristics, they also account for the characteristics of good prose in general, from single chapters to complete books. The preceding analysis based on the concept of term dominance—attained when a term occupies concurrently the paragraph's most important semantic and syntactic positions—is primarily grammatical, and thus offers a means for describing the textual conditions and linguistic cues that produce the internal paragraph relations described by Becker and Christensen. The analysis has also attempted to address the pragmatic and transactional aspects of cohesion by suggesting how inference chains are constructed, and by considering how paragraphs may instantiate the paradigm only imperfectly. Finally, insofar as the analysis captures structural similarities among traditionally differentiated forms such as paragraphs of description, exemplification, or definition, it allows for finer discriminations between textual units than we have been accustomed to make.

5

Multiple Chain Paragraphs

WHILE CHAPTER 4 DEVELOPED THE PARADIGM OF THE SERIES united by a common term as a self-sufficient unit, this chapter will explore the ways in which equivalence chains are conjoined or embedded within one another to form more complex paragraph structures.

The immediate ramifications for a cohesion study are several. First, the conjoinment of two units necessarily entails two equivalence chains, and the number of chains will increase with the number of units conjoined or embedded within one another. Thus, not only must the relations of items within each chain be accounted for, but also the relations between the chains themselves. Also, the presence of more than one equivalence chain requires an extension of the definition of dominance developed in chapter 4, since that definition was predicated on the single-term chain. As will be shown shortly, the presence of multiple chains can and does give rise to topic sentences, which is not possible for the single series. Finally, in paragraphs with topic sentences, the relationships between items within a single chain will necessarily be more complex and varied than the simple identity and reference relationships in the single-term paragraph. If one imagines the topic sentence as the most general sentence of a paragraph, then individual items in chains will perforce reflect a general-to-specific relationship.

The Double Series Paragraph

To illustrate the concept of conjoined chains, we can begin with a paragraph which represents its simplest manifestation:

John likes Columbus. He likes its low inflation rate and its very low crime rate. He enjoys its many foreign food stores. He likes the city's extensive park system. Finally, he likes the cultural and sporting events that the city provides.

The first equivalence chain, the "John" chain, is easily and immediately identified within the framework described in chapter 4. "John," or an equivalent pronoun, appears in each sentence and occupies the dominant noun phrase position. The second chain, "Columbus," is instantiated through "its" and "city," and also occurs in each sentence. A third possible chain is the verb sequence, but it does not constitute the same kind of equivalence chain as a noun sequence, since verbs lack antecedents and referents. Verbs obviously perform the actual conjoining of equivalence chains, and thus contribute to cohesion, but here we must focus on the noun equivalences.

In illustrating the basic paradigm for two conjoined chains, the "John likes Columbus" paragraph also exhibits a straightforward, noncontroversial topic sentence, the kind Braddock in his study labeled "simple": a stated and complete T-unit representing the main idea of the paragraph.[1] In this instance, the topic sentence also enables us to extend our definition of dominance. Chapter 4 showed how the mere presence of a repeated term in each sentence will not insure unity or cohesion, and now we can see that neither will the presence of two repeated terms in each sentence:

John likes Columbus. He likes its low crime rate and its low inflation rate. Someone told John that Columbus is located in the geographic middle of Ohio. While visiting friends in Columbus, John saw a Clippers' game last summer. Woody Hayes bumped into John at the Columbus Civic Center.

To insure term dominance and hence unity and cohesion, (1) the two terms must appear in, or be inferrable from, each sentence, and (2) one term must appear consistently in the sentences' subject position and the other in the sentences' object position, i.e., the dominant noun phrase constituent for the predicate. (In a deep structure analysis, "its" dominates "low crime rate" and "low inflation rate.") These conditions merely extend the definition of single-term dominance by incorporating the second and syntactically equal noun phrase in a subject/verb/object (SVO) construction when that noun phrase participates in an equivalence chain. Schematically, the pattern might be represented as follows:

$$
\begin{array}{lll}
A & \text{verb} & B \\
A^2 & \text{verb} & B^2 \\
A^3 & \text{verb} & B^3 \\
A^n & \text{verb} & B^n
\end{array}
$$

The schema graphically depicts a pure double chain paragraph. The first or "John" chain fulfills all the requirements for a single series paragraph. The second or "Columbus" chain, although it occurs in the object position, also appears in each sentence and dominates the subsequent predicate material. It fulfills the single series criteria from the object position; by itself, the "Columbus" chain would form a single series paragraph.

This extended definition of dominance reveals additional evidence for cohesion as a condition attained by the merger of syntactic and semantic elements, rather than as an exclusively semantic condition. If cohesion were purely semantic, then the second version of the "John likes Columbus" paragraph would be cohesive simply because each sentence contains the two repeated items. Here again, any study that presents cohesion as simply definable by recurrences will be producing word lists without describing cohesion.

When the definition of dominance incorporates syntactical relationships, the first sentence of the original version of "John likes Columbus" can be seen as dominating the support sentences syntactically as well as semantically through the set-relations between "Columbus" and "characteristics of Columbus." This combined dominance gives us a syntactic explanation for why the reader interprets "John likes Columbus," rather than one of the support sentences, as the paragraph's topic sentence.

Rarely, however, do authors construct such over-cued texts; usually some form of discourse ellipsis is applied to one of the chains, so that the example paragraph might read:

John likes Columbus. One reason is its low crime rate and very low inflation rate. Another is its many foreign food stores. It also has an extensive city park system. Finally, it offers many cultural and sporting events.

A still more elliptical version might be:

John likes Columbus. It has a low crime rate and a very low inflation rate. It has many foreign food stores. It also has an extensive city park system. Finally, it provides many cultural and sporting events.

In the first version, the transition words, "one reason," "another," "also," and "finally," operate at the paragraph level much like the substitute "one" at the sentence level, and serve as placeholders for "John likes Columbus" so that the equivalence chain can be maintained. Comprehension is not impeded because each sentence is prefaced by a word or phrase that can be interpreted through back anaphora to "John likes Columbus." However, in the second version, reader comprehension depends less on the text itself than on the reader's general world knowledge and inferencing ability. By erasing the "John" chain, the author is depending on the reader to preface each support sentence with an inferential "One reason why John likes Columbus." The content necessary for the inference is not supplied by the text but by the reader's world knowledge— which the author assumes to be shared between the two of them. If the author assumes inaccurately the kind or amount of shared world knowledge and builds a text around this misconception, the reader will not find the passage satisfactorily cohesive:

John likes Columbus. One reason is its low crime rate and very low inflation rate. Another is that it's located in the geographic center of Ohio. Finally, it has a population of 500,000.

This version indicates that in addition to fulfilling the semantic/syntactic criteria for dominance, a double series text must meet another criterion in order to become fully cohesive. It must support an inference chain through which, in this example, the reader can classify all the named characteristics of Columbus in the general category of "likeable characteristics." Unless the author can safely assume that the reader will find geographic centrality and the size of population likeable, the text will not be cohesive despite its clear pattern of semantic/syntactic dominance. The information predicated to the text's second equivalence chain must satisfy, either directly or inferentially, the reader's conception of the argument created by the conjoined chains of "John likes Columbus"—or in other words, the topic sentence. It is here, at the ultimate inference chain latent in any text, that language operates truly as an interface: a path of connection between unique and discrete individuals. At this juncture the author gives the text over to the reader.

The Recurrence Chain Plus Inference Chain Paragraph

As suggested earlier, "John likes Columbus," through its relations with the paragraph's subsequent sentences, represents what Braddock considers a simple topic sentence. Although he does not develop subcategories, a second kind of simple topic sentence does exist: the set-relation statement illustrated by "Felix Smith is a poor basketball coach" instead of the argument statement illustrated by "John likes Columbus." While functionally identical in the sense that both kinds of statements can summarize a paragraph's theme, the set-relation topic sentence exacts different cohesion and inference requirements. Here again is the "John likes Columbus" paragraph, followed by a corresponding set-relation paragraph:

John likes Columbus. One reason is its low crime rate and very low inflation rate. Another is its many foreign food stores. It also has an extensive city park system. Finally, it offers many cultural and sporting events.

Felix Smith is a poor basketball coach. One reason is that he is consistently outcoached in important games. Another is that he doesn't use his players to their full potentials. Also, he can't teach offense. Finally, he relies strictly on man-to-man defense.

In both examples, two equivalence chains are established; and in both, the transition words, "one reason," "another," "also," and "finally," create the first chain. But in the Smith paragraph the second chain, "Felix Smith," comes from the subject position of the topic sentence, whereas in the John paragraph, the second chain, "Co-

lumbus," comes from the object position in the sentence. As a result, the predicate material in the Smith paragraph—"poor basketball coach," "players," "offense," and "man-to-man defense"—does
not form a straightforward equivalence chain but, rather, an inference chain. Unlike the "John" paragraph, the "Smith" paragraph
is not a pure double series paragraph; the inferentially related,
rather than equivalent, nouns in its predicate material could not by
themselves form a single series paragraph as they do in the "John
likes Columbus" paragraph.

The role of the inference chain is made clearest by the following,
skeletal version of the Smith paragraph, which indicates how the
set-relation totality is defined by an equivalence chain and an inference chain, in contrast to the argument totality defined by two
equivalence chains:

> Felix Smith is a poor basketball coach. He is consistently out-
> coached in important games. He doesn't use his players to their
> full potentials. He can't teach offense. Finally, he relies strictly on
> man-to-man defense.

Without any conscious awareness of the process involved, a reader
who accepts the Felix Smith paragraph as cohesive brings considerable world knowledge to bear on the passage and transforms that
knowledge into proposition-relating inferences. No doubt many potential inference sequences exist—"Felix Smith is a poor basketball
coach; Basketball is a game; Felix Smith is consistently outcoached
in important games"—and it would be revealing to test different
readers to determine which inferences they actually make. But
even without such evidence we can reasonably suppose that "poor
basketball coach" is the core of the most probable inference chain:

> Felix Smith is a poor basketball coach. A poor basketball coach is
> consistently outcoached in important games. Felix Smith is con-
> sistently outcoached in important games. A poor basketball coach
> doesn't use his players to their full potentials. Felix Smith doesn't
> use his players to their full potentials. (And so on.)

It is this multiple-step process of drawing on world knowledge
and shaping it into an acceptable inference that finally gives cohesion to the passage. If the necessary inference is not acceptable in
terms of the reader's world knowledge, the passage will not be fully
cohesive:

Felix Smith is a poor basketball coach. He is consistently out-coached in important games. He doesn't use his players to their full potentials. He likes ice cream. He is a Mormon.

Basketball fans, and—one hopes—readers in general, will not find this paragraph cohesive because the last two required inferences are not in accord with our world knowledge that liking ice cream or being a Mormon has nothing to do with coaching. In the set-relation paragraph as in the argument paragraph, the reader's willingness to accept the necessary inferences as true is the final requirement for a cohesive text. Although the reader's decision in that respect is mainly pragmatic, it can also be influenced by one additional feature of the text itself. What seems textually to predict the acceptability of inferences is whether the second inference chain can be formed from the reader's simple dictionary knowledge of terms in the predicate. In this instance, knowing the dictionary definition of coach as "a person who trains athletes or athletic teams," and of basketball as "a game played between two teams of five players each, the object being to throw the ball through an elevated basket on the opponent's side of the rectangular court," enables the reader to set up a second inference chain connecting nouns in the sentence predicates; for example, "Basketball is a game," linking sentence one with sentence two; "Basketball is played with five members per team," linking sentence one with sentence three; "A coach trains players," again linking sentence one with sentence three. By contrast, dictionary knowledge of "ice cream" or of "Mormon" fails to provide the reader with any term that these terms might share with "basketball coach." That individual readers' inferences may vary seems less important than the fact that the text itself limits the possibilities and protects itself from being subjected exclusively to the reader and the world of pragmatics.

That the second inference chain can be established through dictionary knowledge of "basketball coach" helps explain why the reader interprets the first sentence, "Felix Smith is a poor basketball coach," as a topic sentence. Although "basketball coach" is not repeated in each sentence, the phrase's dictionary definition provides the implied premises that connect it with other predicate nominatives. This implied repetition of "basketball coach," along with the explicit repetition of "Felix Smith," establish the two semantically dominant terms in the paragraph, and their consistent recurrence in either the subject or the predicate nominative position establishes their syntactic dominance. This congruence between syntactic and semantic importance fulfills the criteria for cohesion and operationally constitutes the conjoined terms as the paragraph's topic sentence.

As both the Smith and the John paragraphs have illustrated, inference chains represent the last and most critical links among author, text, and reader. In these examples, at least two kinds of inferential relationships are involved. There are, first, the presumed logical relationships between entire sentences, as in the relationship between "Felix Smith is a poor basketball coach" and "He is consistently outcoached in important games." Cohesion requires that the second sentence be interpreted as a "reason." Second, there is the truth value of the first set of relationships, that is, the world knowledge that being outcoached in important games characterizes poor coaching in general and Smith's coaching in particular. Since evoking these appropriate inferences establishes both a text's cohesion and its general communicative success, authors regularly incorporate inference constraints into a paragraph's basic structure. Reproduced below is a paragraph illustrating these textual constraints:

> The reasons our opossum has survived in definitely hostile surroundings for 70 million years are evident. One is his small size: small animals always find hiding places, they always find a little food, where the big ones starve. Another of its assets was its astounding fecundity: if local catastrophes left only a few survivors, it did not take long to re-establish a thriving population. Also the individual opossum is not exactly delicate: it can stand severe punishment—during which it "plays 'possum" and then scampers away—and it can go without food for a considerable time. Finally, a great many different things are "food" to an opossum. Each of these traits has a high survival value, and their combination has presented the United States with a survivor from the Age of Reptiles.[2]

In terms of its kind and number of equivalence chains, this is a set-relation paragraph; its basic structure involves one substantive equivalence chain, "opossum," and one inference chain, "survival traits." A second equivalence chain, "reasons," alluded to in earlier pages as a simple equivalence chain, is actually an interpretive rather than substantive equivalence chain, composed of logical connectors rather than purely lexical items. Syntactically dominant through its appearances in either subject position or sentence modifier position, this interpretive chain dominates the total unit comprised by the "opossum" chain conjoined with the "survival trait" chain. It instructs the reader explicitly how to interpret the conjoined chains, and to emphasize this instruction, the author buttresses the dictionary-based inferences connecting traits with survival by explicit enthymemes: "One is his small size; small animals can always find a little food," and so on.

As a relevant sidenote, one of these supporting enthymemes manifests itself as a version of the double series paradigm:

Also the individual opossum is not exactly delicate: it can stand severe punishment—during which it "plays 'possum" and then scampers away—and it can go without food for a considerable time.

Here the author inserts a mini-topic sentence in the middle of the paragraph. (Since the sentence is headed by the dominating "also," which links it back to the paragraph's topic sentence, the reader is blocked from interpreting this sentence as a topic sentence.) Just as the single series paradigm can be a subunit within more complex paragraphs, so, too, can the double series paradigm. It is thus another instance of Barthes' concept of kernels and satellites, which assumes the existence of defining structures, but also assumes that the size of those structures (in this instance, the number of sentences) determines whether they are perceived as major or minor text units.

Schematically, the opossum paragraph might be represented as below, with the proviso that the basic structure can be expanded through embeddings like those discussed above:

$$A \quad (B\ C)$$
$$A_2 \quad (B_2\ C_2)$$
$$A_n \quad (B_n\ C_n)$$

The degree to which this description of cohesion and paragraph structure can be useful, as well as valid, can be seen when the opossum paragraph is contrasted with a student attempt that begins with the same kind of topic sentence:

> Mrs. Smith was my worst teacher in high school because she was a computer-like person. Myself, being a very studious person, though not a genius, like most other people find themselves frustrated when they cannot find the answer to a study problem after a reasonable length of time. I really appreciate a teacher who will take the time and discuss a student's problems with them on a person to person basis. The student is able to relax and probably understand his problem better. My teacher, Mrs. Smith, was all the time spitting out facts and theorems about this and that. Any student who could not understand these facts was bound to experience trouble. I feel that she could have been a much better teacher if only she were a little more personal with her statements. A more relaxed atmosphere in which to study could possibly have resulted.

Instead of appearing as an upsetting jumble, the student paragraph can be viewed through the set-relation paradigm to reveal a kind of off-target logic. Although laden with local recurrences, the paragraph does not establish a primary equivalence chain. More interesting, I think, is that the set-relation paradigm can explain why the necessary chain was not instantiated. In trying to anticipate and bridge the differences between his world knowledge (what he expects teachers to be like) and the reader's world knowledge on that same topic, the student develops the inference chain that explains why Mrs. Smith's characteristics make her a poor teacher, before naming those characteristics. That is, the student tries to develop the inference chain before establishing the equivalence chain.

The opossum paragraph illustrates the explanatory power of the set-relation paradigm in one way. But, in fact, the opossum paragraph is an imperfect, if allowable, instantiation of the paradigm. In the base sentence introducing the three relevant chains, the main verb phrase operates merely as a grammatical placeholder: "The reasons our opossum has survived in definitely hostile surroundings for 70 million years *are evident.*" No chains originate from the verb phrase, although it is, after the subject, a sentence's syntactically most important position. On the other hand, two of the three chains, the opossum and the survival traits, are embedded in the subject phrase, and thus originate from syntactically subordinate positions. This unequal origin of the chains keeps the topic sentence from attaining the complete dominance it could attain with a chain originating from the main verb phrase. A topic sentence which not only fulfills the criteria for dominance, but in so doing more accurately reflects the paragraph's thesis, is "Our opossum has many survival traits," because of its structurally coequal introduction of the two primary chains.

In some cases when the conjoined primary chains are embedded in a syntactic structure such as the subject, the sentence containing that conjoinment may lose its status as the topic sentence:

> The arbitrariness of the structuring of things and thoughts is familiar to anyone who has ever learned a foreign langauge. That continuum of reality which English separates into two units through the labels *arm* and *hand* is treated as a single unit by the Russian label *ruká*. That area of action which English divides into two units through the labels *carry* and *bear* is handled as a single unit by the French *porter*. That area of thought which English treats as a single unit through the label *remember* is divided in German into two units through the one-word label *behalten* ('remember' = 'keep in mind') and the three-word label *sich erinnern an* ('remember' = 'recall to mind').[3]

If a reader views the first sentence as a topic sentence, it is clearly of a different nature from "John likes Columbus"; it does not operate as an overarching sentence for subsequent sentences; rather, it operates as a base sentence from which the others arise. Indeed, one can substantially change the first sentence: "The arbitrariness of the structuring of things and thoughts is the basis for Whorf's theory of language." So drastic a change is possible because no chains in the paragraph track back to the verb phrase of its topic sentence; the main idea of the paragraph is captured in the noun phrase and not the entire sentence.

Whether the conjoined chains are instantiated as an entire paragraph or as a paragraph subunit, the basic grammatical component of the chains is the simple SVO sentence/clause. Psycholinguists have accumulated impressive evidence demonstrating that the clause is the primary perceptual unit because it is the minimal unit with semantic determinacy. "The constituent words of a clause become perceptually determinate only when they are perceived as functional elements within the clause, and these definite functions are fully determined only after the whole clause is perceived."[4]

This chapter's analysis of conjoined chains suggests that the sentence/clause SVO creates a similar determinacy at the discourse level: sentences following the SVO sentence/clause become maximally determinate only when perceived as being dominated by the SVO sentence/clause and fulfilling the criteria for dominance. The conjoined chains in the SVO form are the textual equivalent to the psycholinguists' frame, the rhetoricians' topic sentence, or the structuralists' totality. The conjoined chains in SVO form are the base from which everything else is contextualized and given meaning. This form not only contains the head-words for the subsequent chains, but also constitutes those as a unit; it is the whole into which the parts are fit and understood when all chains lead away from the coinjoined unit and all lead back to it. In this respect, the double series paradigm as defined by dominance represents a convergence of theories derived from structuralism, psycholinguistics, and linguistics. Sentences or sentence constituents which are not incorporated into the recurrence chain disrupt the cohesion of a paragraph; conversely, the degree to which sentences and sentence constituents are incorporated into the recurrence chain reflect the paragraph's cohesion and also its structural pattern. As Culler puts it: "Some Christmas trees are more successful than others, and we are inclined to think that symmetry and harmonious arrangement of ornaments makes some contribution towards success."[5]

The concept of dominance can also be grounded in information theory. It has long been noted that in English there is a general tendency to place shared information—information presumed common to both author and reader—in the sentence initial position, and to place new information in the end position. The conjoined series primary SVO sentence/clause seems to perform this function at the paragraph level, providing in one conjoined unit all the initiating words in the two recurrence chains.

Information theory and inference overloading seem necessary to explain the parameters affecting the relations of items within a single recurrence chain. All the recurrence chains we have examined thus far have been based either on simple coreferentiality instantiated through pronouns, or on the set-relations of HAS:A or

IS:A. Neither of these instantiations really adds new information. However, consider the following hierarchy of more-to-less acceptable instantiations of "Felix Smith" in a recurrence chain:

> Felix Smith is a poor basketball coach.
> *He* is always outcoached in important games.
> The *jerk* is always outcoached . . .
> The *man* is always outcoached . . .
> The *Yale alumnus* is always outcoached . . .
> The *husband* is always outcoached . . .
> The *Rotarian* is always outcoached . . .

Since there is only one available referent, "Felix Smith," for "jerk," "man," "Yale alumnus," "husband," and "Rotarian," unacceptability is not caused by competing or confusing antecedents. The increasing threat to cohesion in the later items seems to result from the amount of new information they introduce; whereas "jerk" is all but implicit in "poor basketball coach," and "man" is implicit in the name "Felix Smith," terms like "Yale alumnus," "husband," and "Rotarian" must be connected with "Felix Smith" by inferences based on the reader's world knowledge. As the reader is required to make these connections, the recurrence chain loses the stability derived from unequivocally shared information; the equivalence chain gets overloaded by the inferences necessary to accommodate new information.

Mixed Chain Paragraphs Without a Topic Sentence

Chapter 4 examined the pure single chain paragraph, and thus far this chapter has examined both the pure double series paragraph and the conjoined equivalence and inference chain paragraph. All these paragraph types are limited and limiting, consisting of fairly simple chains; neither the chains themselves nor their various combinations acommodate much information. Indeed, probably because of this limited information capacity, most paragraphs combine these structural forms and consist of one primary chain and two or three secondary chains that appear in many but not all of a paragraph's sentences. This next section reviews paragraphs of the mixed type.

The mixed form manifests a classic communication problem. In contrast to the earlier types, the mixed form is more informationally rich and characterized by a greater sense of thematic progression, without, however, sacrificing its integrity as a unit. It produces a strong sense of back anaphora, or vertical structuring, as well as a sense of advancing theme, or linear and horizontal structuring. The dynamic juxtaposing and balancing between two potentially conflicting conditions characterizes this paragraph type, whose complex linearity has been a principal impediment to our efforts to describe paragraph cohesion and structure. In a text characterized by thematic progression, the inherent control imposed by a repeated subject no longer exists, since the subjects themselves are continually being replaced. In the absence of alternative controls, the text will not be actualized:

> John likes cheese. Cheese is made in Wisconsin. Wisconsin is the home of my best friend.

Although patently lacking cohesion, this example fulfills Daneš' discourse category of "simple linear progression, in which the rheme of one sentence becomes the theme of the next."[6]

But while Daneš' pattern may describe recurrences, it obviously does not describe cohesion, and we must proceed to identify some other necessary requirements for the linear pattern.

The following is an example of a mixed structure paragraph that employs linear progression:

> Imagine, if you will, a minuscule "chip" shaved from a crystal of silicon. On this chip are all the components of an entire information storage and programming system—a full-fledged computer, in other words, that takes up less space than the first four letters of this paragraph. That is the microcomputer of tomorrow and its prototype already exists. The information it stores could come from anywhere—The Library of Congress, *The New York Times*, the personal banking records of thousands of taxpaying citizens. It could come from the tape cassettes of psychiatrists, the daydreams of novelists, the logbooks of birdwatchers. Soon information of this sort will be available to anyone and everyone at the flick of a switch. You'll be able to plug into it. So will the government. So will the guy next door. Your *kid* will be able to plug into that information—your doctor, your thesis advisor, your guru, your garbage man. And when

everyone is all plugged in and accessing, in unison, this monumental new universe of data, the existential situation is going to change.[7]

In order to identify the underlying patterns of recurrence in this paragraph, the following schema lists the subjects and objects of the paragraph's sentences; such an analysis is consistent with the preceding discussion, which designated subject and object positions as informationally most important:

Subjects	Verbs	Objects or Predicate Nominatives
(You) implied		chip
Chip		components for an entire information storage and programming system
That		microcomputer
Its prototype	exists	
Information		anywhere
It (information)		tape, cassettes, daydreams, etc.
Information		anyone
You		it (information)
Government		(information)
Guy		(information)
Kid		(information)
Situation	is going to change	

This simple list reveals a perhaps startling fact: the basic, dominating recurrence chain, based not only on repetition but also on syntactical position as subject or object, is "information."

While "information" does not occur in each sentence, it does occur in eight of the twelve sentences (counting the compound sentence as two), and it consistently appears in either the subject or the object position. It is thus the only candidate for the primary recurrence chain, fulfilling the criteria for dominance by the congruence between its semantic and syntactic importance. The establishment of this primary recurrence chain is the first requirement for the successful mixed structure paragraph, just as it is the basic requirement for the single series paragraph.

The second requirement of the mixed structure paragraph involves the secondary recurrence chains—their syntactic positions and the means by which they are introduced. Any sequence opening with an item other than "information," or in other words, any opening item other than that of the primary recurrence chain, qualifies for membership in a secondary chain. The most obvious secondary recurrence chain, because of its length, is the "people" chain:

> You'll be able to plug into it. So will the government. So will the guy next door. Your kid will be able to plug into that information —your creditor, your thesis advisor, your guru, your garbage man.

This four-sentence sequence fulfills the basic conditions of a secondary chain, that is, a chain sufficiently different from the primary chain to introduce new information, yet related to the primary chain in such a way that the new information, as it in turn is incorporated in its own recurrence chain, can be interpreted as an extension of the primary recurrence chain rather than as a new and different chain. For that to happen, the secondary recurrence chain should be introduced into the text by the primary chain, as in: "Soon information of this sort will be available to anyone and everyone at the flick of a switch." Second, when an instantiation of the secondary recurrence chain appears in the subject position, an instantiation of the primary recurrence chain should appear in the predicate position, as in: "You'll be able to plug into it (information)." Schematically, the pattern is as follows:

$$A \quad verb \quad B$$
$$B \quad verb \quad A$$

Both of these conditions for introducing secondary chains reflect the necessity of back anaphora to prevent a noncohesive linear progression like the Wisconsin cheese sequence. From an information theory viewpoint, these conditions reveal how new, unknown information—the secondary recurrence chain—is introduced and developed through old, known information without its signaling a new topic or paragraph structure.

In the "chip" paragraph, another candidate for a secondary recurrence chain is found in the following sequence:

> On this chip are the components for an entire information storage and programming system—a full-fledged computer, in other words, that takes up less space than the first four letters of this paragraph. That is the microcomputer of tomorrow and its prototype already exists.

The recurrence pattern for this sequence can be represented as follows:

$$A \quad \text{verb} \quad B$$
$$B \quad \text{verb} \quad C$$

To the extent that the new information about the computer is introduced via old information, the sequence fulfills one of the previously outlined conditions for introducing new information. But because the new information, "microcomputer of tomorrow" and "prototype already exists," is not then incorporated into other chains, and has only one recurrence link, the sentence is of marginal importance informationally and structurally. A sentence with only a single recurrence link can easily be pruned without disrupting either cohesion or sense. It is an allowable aside within the structural and cohesion patterns, but not critical to either.

There are two final issues to be addressed with regard to the relationships in this paragraph between secondary chains and the primary chain: the status of the secondary recurrence of "chip," and the introduction of "information" into the text. Both of these are revealed in the paragraph's first two sentences:

> Imagine, if you will, a minuscule "chip" shaved from a crystal of silicon. On this chip are all the components for an entire information storage and programming system—a full-fledged computer, in other words, that takes up less space than the first four letters of this paragraph.

The pattern of the "chip" recurrence chain duplicates the computer pattern just examined (A verb B; B verb C), and also one of the patterns for the single series paradigm discussed in chapter 4. Informationally, the second sentence introduces both "computer" and "information" to the text, besides other items not chained at all ("programming system," "components," etc.). The sentence is informationally very busy and rhetorically, structurally, full of authorial opportunities and choices. Besides setting up the possible development of "chip" in the form of a single series, it also sets up the possibility of a "computer" chain, as well as the other potential chains just noted. The actualized chain is, of course, the "information" chain, and it emerges from the position of adjective, a minor sentence constituent in surface structure analysis, rather than from the major object position.

However, in a deep structure analysis, adjectives are viewed as NP's, so that the originating structure for "information storage system" is the basic SVO clause, "system stores information," in which "information" occupies the object position in one of the deep structure sentences. Given the various deep-structure constituent sentences of the sentence, "On this chip are all the components of an entire information storage and programming system—a full-fledged computer, in other words, that takes up less space than the first four letters of this paragraph," the author, among several possible choices, could have written this sequence: "On the chip are components; the components are for a system; the system stores information; the system programs information." Thus, although in the surface structure "information" is in the subordinate adjective position, by deep structure definition it has the potential to be actualized as an object. And it is precisely because "information" can be actualized as an object that its eventual role as a primary recurrence chain is predictable.

Finally, among texts which synthesize information by combining SVO clauses into complex sentences, those that maintain the primacy of the SVO clause will be more cohesive than those which do not. That is, texts whose recurrence chain items can be derived from a deep-structure SVO sentence/clause and which, furthermore, preserve and maintain that SVO derivation in their surface manifestations, will be more cohesive than texts whose recurrences either lack such a derivation or have it obscured by inconsistent surface manifestations.

One can contrast the cohesive use of primary and secondary chains in the "information" paragraph with the following weakly cohesive student text that violates the rules just outlined:

The book *Who's Who in Engineering* is an index of engineers and engineering societies in the United States. The American Association of Engineering Societies (AAES) compiled the data used in the book. The book starts with the criteria for being placed in the index. The names and positions of the governing body of the AAES are presented and the member societies, associate societies, and regional societies are listed. The different engineering societies and organizations and engineering awards are indexed separately. The major engineering societies are listed with the officers' names, the award they give, and the past recipients of the awards. The engineers are listed in alphabetical order with a small profile on each. At the end of the book engineers are indexed geographically and by area of specialization.

In skeletal, SVO form, the paragraph can be schematized as follows:

Subjects	Verbs	Objects
book	is	index
AAES	compiled	data
book	starts with	criteria
names and positions	are presented	
member societies, associate societies, regional societies	are listed	
different engineering societies and organizations and engineering awards	are indexed	
engineering societies	are listed	
engineers	are listed	
engineers	are indexed	

Although "book" (or "index") would seem an obvious choice for the primary recurrence chain, it never gains textual instantiation because of the many competing items in subject positions: "AAES," "names and positions," "engineering societies," and "engineers." Besides this competition, "book" also loses thematic and cohesive status by its inconsistent placement in sentence two. After first being introduced as a subject in sentence one, "book" is demoted to the status of a non-SVO prepositional phrase in sentence two, "in the book."

With such a weak and doubtful primary chain, the burden for cohesion would seem to fall on the secondary chains. But here again the recurrences are basically helter-skelter: sentence subjects, and thus potential recurrence chains, are not introduced by preceding sentences and thus lack that immediate back anaphora inherent in the A : B; B : A pattern. A very likely prospect for a secondary chain, "AAES," introduced in the subject position of the second sentence, is simply banished from the text entirely. Like the demotion of "book," the disappearance of "AAES" reflects the text's failure to respect and maintain the integrity of an SVO component, and thus its capacity to enhance cohesion. The following passage illustrates the latent cohesive power of "AAES" when it fulfills its potential as a secondary recurrence chain:

> The names and positions of the governing body of the AAES are presented and *its* member societies, associate societies, and regional societies are listed. *Non-AAES* engineering societies and organizations and their awards are listed separately.

While the original passage invites more discussion (and more editing), I will make only one final observation. Although not as inherently evil as most composition texts suggest, the passive sentence construction, which this paragraph used extensively in elliptic form, is probably the primary source of the overall weak cohesion. In an elliptic form where the presumed agents are not named, the passive constructions effectively stripped deep-structure SVO units of their subjects, and produced the following sentences:

> Names and positions . . . are presented and member societies . . . are listed. The different engineering societies . . . are indexed separately.

Lacking surface objects, the sentences distort their deep-structure SVO patterns and prevent the instantiation of the A : B; B : A pattern by deleting both the potential recurrence chain item and its syntactic position. Once again, not only is the importance to cohesion of syntax confirmed, but also the importance of surface syntax.

In summary, the last few pages have examined the interactions between recurrence chains. As the texts themselves have become more complex, so, too, has the definition of dominance, but the definition has been extended according to its original logic, not by ad hoc qualifications. The criterion for dominance is always congruence between semantic importance and syntactic importance. In the single series, dominance is attained by the chain's appearing in the subject position; in the double series, by the two chains' appearing repeatedly in the subject and object positions. In the mixed paradigm, first, the primary chain must regularly appear in either the subject or object position; second, the secondary chains must be introduced through a sentence containing the primary chain; and finally, item recurrences must reflect their derivational history from an SVO sentence/clause.

Mixed Chain Paragraphs with a Topic Sentence

The "information" paragraph just examined is a mixed sequence paragraph without a topic sentence. Our sense that it lacks a topic sentence results from the A:B; B:A pattern by which the secondary chains were introduced as the linear progression led from "chip" to "information" to "people." Because all the chains were introduced through discrete and separate sentences, no one topic sentence emerged. Our sense of a topic sentence is fulfilled, however, when all the secondary chains are introduced through reduced SVO clauses that, in turn, are combined with the primary chain into a single unit, a single sentence. We can see that happening in the following paragraph:

> In regard to the use of space, it is possible to observe a basic and sometimes inexplicable dichotomy in the animal world. Some species huddle together and require contact with each other. Others completely avoid touching. No apparent logic governs the category into which a species falls. Contact creatures include the walrus, the hippopotamus, the pig, the brown bat, the parakeet, and the hedgehog among many other species. The horse, the dog, the cat, the rat, the muskrat, the hawk, and the black-headed gull are non-contact species. Curiously enough, closely related animals may belong to different categories. The great Emperor penguin is a contact species. It conserves heat through contact with its fellows by huddling together in large groups and thus increases its adaptability to cold. Its range extends over many parts of Antarctica. The smaller Adelíe penguin is a non-contact species. Thus it is somewhat less

adaptable to cold than the Emperor, and its range is apparently more limited.[8]

Instead of introducing secondary chains through the object position, as the "information" paragraph did, this text presents them through reduced SVO forms which are then immediatley combined into the first, complex sentence of the paragraph. Instead of "The dichotomy is basic; The dichotomy is also inexplicable," occurring as separate items, these two SVO's are combined into "a basic and inexplicable dichotomy."

Just as the SVO clauses are reduced and synthesized into a single opening sentence, the remainder of the paragraph plucks out each reduced SVO from the first sentence, restores it to full SVO status, and proceeds to develop it individually. Thus from the perspective of reduced-to-restored SVO's, the core sentences of the paragraph are:

No apparent logic governs the category into which an animal falls.

Curiously enough, closely related animals may belong to different categories.

As this list suggests, the shared recurrence is the chain of "dichotomy" from the first sentence, and "category" from the fourth; these two core sentences provide the single "dichotomy: category" chain. The chain's semantic importance, attained through repetition, is congruent with its syntactic importance, attained through the chain's consistent appearances in the sentences' object positions. This condition of limited dominance, taken in conjunction with the means by which SVO's are expanded and the manner in which they operate in the text, make the chain, "dichotomy:category," the primary recurrence chain in the paragraph.

First, each expanded SVO operates as a mini-topic sentence, as in the sequence:

No apparent logic governs the category into which a species falls. Contact creatures include the walrus, the hippopotamus, the pig, the brown bat, the parakeet, and the hedgehog among many other species. The horse, the dog, the cat, the rat, the muskrat, the hawk, and the black-headed gull are non-contact creatures.

Both in this and the other SVO sequence, "category" and its subject (either "no apparent logic" or "closely related animals") contextually frame their succeeding sentences. In turn, these core sentences, under a reduced-to-restored analysis, are dominated by the first sentence of the paragraph. Finally, because of this hierarchy of dominance, within which "category" occupies the object position of each core sentence and "dichotomy" the object position of the first sentence, the "category:dichotomy" chain emerges as the primary recurrence chain, and the opening sentence as the topic sentence.

Also supporting these two perceptions is the manner in which the mini-topic sentence segments are developed. Instead of relying solely on single-term repetition, the chains in this paragraph move from general to specific instantiations: dichotomy to category; animal world to species to particular animals. With a text employing this kind of chain instantiation, our sense of topic sentence and primary recurrence chain is shaped by a semantic relation other than simple repetition; instead, it is shaped by the set-relations of class/member, so that the "class" items are seen as encompassing the member items. Here, once again, the paragraph's initial sentence contains the most general class instantiations of the recurrence chains, and that also leads it to be interpreted as the paragraph's topic sentence.

Conclusions and Implications

In conclusion, this chapter has examined some of the conditions under which recurrence chains interact with one another to form informationally rich and complex paragraphs. Building on the basic definition of cohesion as term dominance, the chapter posited three potential elaborations of the single recurrence chain: the pure double series, the recurrence chain plus inference chain, and the mixed sequence based on primary and secondary chains. As the number and kind of recurrence chains grew, the contributions of syntax likewise increased, from first simply establishing a chain by insuring congruence between a term's semantic and syntactic importance to then adjudicating among the chains' interrelationships by signaling either their coordinate or subordinate status. Because of the ensuing syntactical hierarchy, patterns of recurrence chains are formed, and structures delinated, so that paragraph juncture becomes predicable.

Although not yet empirically tested, the two most stable patterns seem to be the series united by the common term and the mixed sequence with reduced SVO's. The series united by a common term seems to be the building block of many paragraphs such as the "information" paragraph which conjoins these series to create a more complex structure. The degree to which readers find that conjoined paradigm acceptable as a unit deserves empirical testing. One might predict that mixed sequences are most susceptible to segmenting into single series paragraphs. The strongest constraint on such segmenting would probably be the number of recurrence chains involved, or the use of text-dependent phrases such as "this . . . ," or "others . . . ," which must be interpreted through back anaphora.

Empirical investigation might also show whether the mixed sequence based on the double series is the next most stable unit because of its use of reduced-to-restored SVO's, which tie subsequent sentences to the initial sentence containing the reduced SVO's. Recognition of this pattern, however, would presumably be affected as well by the length of development of the restored SVO's or minitopic sentences; if the restored SVO's in the animal paragraph, for example, had been developed through 10 or 12 sentences, the paragraph's mere length might have called for a paragraph juncture— especially in a popular article.

Besides describing paragraph structure, the preceding analysis accounts for both the horizontal thematic progression and the vertical deepening inherent in discourse. The specific means here examined were the conjoined subject/predicate, or A : B (where B introduces new information), and the embedded reduced-to-restored SVO's. On the one hand, each of these is a single unit signaled by its syntactic conjoinment, and thus constitutes the psychological frame (or the rhetoricians' base sentence) from which other sentences arise. On the other hand, each can be combined with another unit to provide the means by which new information is introduced to create thematic progression.

Finally, the implications of the preceding analysis must be examined from the perspective of the much beleaguered topic sentence. Like chapter 4 in its examination of the single series paradigm, this chapter examined a paragraph type that can be cohesive, elegant, and also lacking a topic sentence. The functional, structural, and informational necessity for a topic sentence once again depends primarily on the informational purpose of the message. Even among paragraphs with topic sentences, there are distinctions in both form and development, so that the simple argument topic sentence, "John likes Columbus," and the simple set-relation topic sentence, "Felix Smith is a poor basketball coach," have different information and inference requirements and are developed by different kinds of recurrence and inference chains. Furthermore, as the analysis of complex paragraphs showed, topic sentences, operationally defined through the concept of dominance, can and do appear within paragraphs. The overreaching conclusion to be drawn is that the topic sentence is merely *one* means by which information is conjoined and combined. It does provide the reader with a contextual frame that allows for the integration of subsequent information, but so, too, does a base sentence sequence (A:B; B:A). The fundamental appeal of the topic sentence is its structural tidiness; that is, paragraphs with topic sentences are characterized by the more controlled, tighter recurrence chains that are "umbrellaed" under the topic sentence.

Conversely, paragraphs with a base sentence sequence rather than a topic sentence lack this umbrella effect; all chains do not emanate from, or lead back to, a single sentence. Although one might argue that a topic sentence is intrinsically richer and more complex than a base sentence, it may not always be more effective from a message point of view. By definition, the topic sentence paragraph develops at least two recurrence chains simultaneously, and thus requires more attention and processing ability from the reader. In technical or scientific writing dealing with esoteric or complex topics, the base sentence structure may indeed be more appropriate because it is characterized by the sequential joining of single-term sequences. What the topic sentence presents as a single unit, the base sentence sequence breaks up into more easily understood segments, which are developed individually before they are linked with other segments. Thus the two types of paragraphs serve different informational needs, and the structural elegance of the topic sentence paragraph does not make it intrinsically "superior" to the base sentence sequence paragraph.

6

Implications and Applications

WHERE MUCH CURRENT RESEARCH OCCUPIES ITSELF WITH PRO-
cess, the preceding chapters have doggedly (although I hope not
perversely) examined one of the products of the composing process—the enigmatic expository English paragraph. These chapters
have argued for a description of both paragraph form and paragraph
cohesion based on the concept of the dominant recurring term. Seen
as an informing superordinate, the dominant term is compatible
with the psychologists' frame and the rhetoricians' topic sentence,
and it offers both rhetoricians and composition teachers a formal and
publicly accessible avenue to those notions. Heavily grounded in
syntactic analysis, my definition of dominance helps penetrate the
traditional and exclusively semantic definition of the paragraph as
the development of a complete idea. Instead it offers four possible,
although not exhaustive, patterns for expository paragraphs: the
single series united by a common term; the double series united by
two common terms; the double series united by one recurrence
chain and one inference chain; and the mixed series based on combinations of the single and double series.

Comparisons With Other Approaches

To the extent that the analysis relies on current linguistic theory
in its sentence parsing, the process of establishing the syntactic
position of each recurrence item is straightforward and reproduc-

ible. The limitation of the analysis is that it cannot track the recurrences themselves in an equally straightforward and reproducible manner. Paragraphs with highly visible and highly referential recurrence chains were used to illustrate the basic paradigms; but language is considerably more rich and poetic than the one-to-one referentiality of nouns and pronouns. As indicated in chapter 1, current semantic theories offer little or no help in describing the rich allusiveness of language.

Despite such limitations, the anlaysis of cohesion presented here produces, I believe, a more accurate description of discourse than the two most currently popular approaches: Kintsch's propositional analysis and Francis Christensen's generative rhetoric. As noted in chapter 3, Kintsch analyzes discourse into what he calls propositions, which, for all intents and purposes, are surface structure constituents:

John sleeps.	(sleep, John)
The man is sick.	(sick, man)
The old man smiled and	(old, man) & (smile, man)
left the room.	& (Leave, man, room)[1]

These propositions are then ordered by the (A, B) (B, C) chronology, so that proposition (A, B) is superordinate to proposition (B, C) because (A, B) precedes (B, C) and shares with it the common argument B. Thus in a Kintschian analysis, a sample sentence is segmented as follows:

A great black and yellow V-2 rocket forty-six
feet long stood in a New Mexico desert.

1 (GREAT, ROCKET)
2 (BLACK, ROCKET)
3 (YELLOW, ROCKET)
4 (V-2, ROCKET)
5 (LONG, ROCKET)
6 (FORTY-SIX FEET, 5)
7 (STAND, ROCKET)
8 (IN, 7, DESERT)
9 (NEW MEXICO, DESERT)

These propositions are then schematized[2] as follows:

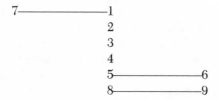

This characteristic analysis shows how Kintsch's method is based on a contradiction; it uses surface structure constituents but at the same time masks and ignores their capacity to manifest the actual relationships involved in cohesion; surface relationships are homogenized into the simple propositional relationship. This failure, combined with Kintsch's ranking of propositions through shared terms, disables his analysis from dealing with such double chain sequences as "John likes Columbus; He likes its park system." His system can define only a single linear relationship; it can neither identify nor describe the double recurrence chains of "John" and "Columbus." Conversely, Kintsch's system cannot fault the sequence: "John likes cheese; Cheese is made in Wisconsin; Wisconsin is a cold state" simply because the sequence includes the recurrences of "cheese" and "Wisconsin." Kintsch offers no criteria other than simple repetition by which to evaluate the introduction of new information.

Christensen's method suffers from essentially the same weaknesses. Christensen posits two possible relationships between sentences: subordination and coordination. These are signaled by and manifested by a single recurrence chain, so that Christensen's method, like Kintsch's, cannot deal with double recurrence chains, their relationships, or their contribution to cohesion. Below is a sample paragraph analyzed by Christensen's method in which coordinate sentences are ranked at the same level and subordinate sentences are ranked at a new level:

1. The process of learning is essential to our lives.

2. All higher animals seek it deliberately.

3. They are inquisitive and they experiment.

4. An experiment is a sort of harmless trial run of some action which we shall have to make in the real world; and this,

whether it is made in the laboratory by scientists or by fox-
cubs outside their earth.

5. The scientist experiments and the cub plays; both are
   learning to correct their errors of judgment in a setting in
   which the errors are not fatal.

6. Perhaps this is what gives them both their air of happi-
   ness and freedom in these activities.[3]

In Christensen's analysis, the above paragraph is based solely on
subordination, and the strong back anaphora created by the chains
of "learning" and "higher animals" that actually unifies the text is
entirely ignored.

The analysis presented in the preceding chapters, because it is
based on the interactive contributions of both syntax and semantics,
lays the ground for identifying and describing patterned double and
triple recurrence chains. The "learning" paragraph cited above exhibits the same A:B, B:A pattern seen in the "information" paragraph analyzed in chapter 5—a common pattern that forestalls the
runaway "Wisconsin cheese" sequences. But the analysis in that
chapter does not presuppose a single set of relationships and does
not ignore or mask complex relationships.

Finally, I think my analysis has remained sensitive to one of the
most basic tenets of discourse, that sentences which individually are
grammatically correct may not remain so in particular contexts, and
its corollary, that sentences derive their semantic and syntactic con-
figurations from the context in which they appear. In this respect
the analysis begins to account for some of the most important conditions of discourse: that the whole is larger than the sum of its parts,
that a text is always an interface between worlds of knowledge, and
that successful texts take these conditions into account.

In attempting to identify some of the psychological and metalin-
guistic considerations that influence paragraph structure, my analysis also tries to bridge the gap between a Rogerian conception of the
paragraph as an exclusively discourse structure and a Christensen/
Becker conception of the paragraph as a formal structure. I think
it is of enormous significance that both Christensen's "Generative
Rhetoric of the Paragraph" and Rogers' "Discourse-Centered Rhetoric of the Paragraph" begin by arguing the inadequacy of the traditional definition of the paragraph as simply the development of a

single idea.[4] Of course, both pursue their arguments to different conclusions—Rogers to his conception of the paragraph as a "discourse stadium" and Christensen to his famous generative rhetoric. But as the debate hammered home, the paragraph in its traditional, wholly semantic definition as the development of a single and complete idea will always be an easy victim to theories of intuition. Like an unenforceable law, this definition invites its own violation, and we see the grisly evidence all around us. On the one hand, paragraphs have become austere readability measures by which the groping intuition of the least able reader sets the standard for the majority. On the other hand, they have become baroque labyrinths in which the self-indulgent intuition of a Paul de Man paragraph could care less about offering the reader a breath of white space.

Yet there is something fundamentally right, and impossible to discard, in the traditional definition of the paragraph as the development of a single idea, which has enabled it to survive innumerable qualifications and sustain thousands of composition classes and millions of readers. My analysis has tried to preserve this basic rightness, while refining and formalizing the traditional definition in a reproducible manner. It has assumed that the territory is there but not yet fully mapped, and it has tried to map four syntactically informed alternatives for developing the wholly semantic "single and complete idea." It has described what seems to be a quite basic paradigm—the single-term series—both as a self-sufficient unit and as a potential subunit in larger, more complex paragraph units. In demonstrating the capacity of the single series to become either a whole or a part, my analysis speaks to Christensen's formalism in which the paragraph is treated as a self-contained discourse unit; it speaks at the same time to Rogers' intuitional reminder that paragraphs are also but parts in a larger whole.

Classroom Applications

I would like to think that the applications to composition teaching are obvious. The most immediate is that the analysis provides a formal and reproducible model for teachers and students. Like current sentence-combining techniques, the paragraph patterns I have described are definable and discrete models for packaging sentence sequences into unified texts at the discourse level. Their underlying theory assumes only a rudimentary grasp of grammar, and its application requires neither elaborate techniques of analysis nor the mastery of obscure terminology. The only abilities required are the recognizing of subjects and objects and the counting of their instantiations. In these resepcts the theory meets two widely accepted criteria of effective pedagogy: that students respond positively to models, and that teachers should meet students where they are, should begin with students' present knowledge and then enlarge that knowledge into a more conscious awareness of discourse structure.

Depending on the students' particular needs, the models can function either as generative devices, or as evaluative, editing devices. As generative devices they offer the student patterns for combining sentence sequences, yet patterns that are at the same time free of text. I explain. Students, after all, may respond to models only too well: the weakest and least confident student writers—the ones most important to the teacher—tend all too often to imitate models slavishly rather than to assimilate them conceptually. If the possibility is left open to do so, these students will turn composition exercises into mechanical performances equivalent to typing or penmanship practice. But text-free models, even in their most slavish and mechanical imitations, require thought and input from the students, i.e., composition.

The analysis also presents a spectrum of continuous and cumulative structures, from simple to complex, that enables the teacher for the first time to present discourse structures in a logically graduated fashion, as in the teaching of mathematics and some of the sciences. In the traditional teaching of composition, the only progression is the basically modal progression from description to narration to analysis to argumentation. But a theme must achieve cohesion whether it is descriptive or argumentative, so that the patterns analyzed here impart skills that precede, logically and pedagogically, the skills necessary to produce the rhetorical modes of discourse.

In this way the patterns speak to one of the most common failures in student writing: the mechanically "coherent" but woefully disunified paragraph that the student wrote in the Ohio Union that is on the Olentangy River that flows through Columbus that really carried her away—the paragraph that begins in Poughkeepsie and ends in Albuquerque because of the student's microscopic, deconstructed concept of the paragraph as a totality. As Piaget has written, one aspect of maturing involves the widening of perception from a personal and egocentric world view to a social world view. And as composition teachers have noted, one of the biggest hurdles for beginning writers to overcome is the qualitative difference between cohesive—flowing river—oral discourse and cohesive written discourse. These patterns provide one means for immature writers to develop the broader and more structured view necessary to written texts.

The usefulness of the models as evaluative or editing devices has already been suggested by the analyses of the student texts on the poor teacher and the AAES index in chapter 5. The models can provide teachers and students with a specific and relatively nonthreatening vocabulary for criticism and instruction. Instead of criticizing a student paragraph in generalized, subjective terms for lack of cohesion—a criticism which can be taken personally and defensively—the teacher using these models has a means of reasoning with the student and raising the level of discussion from personal criticism to the sharing of a common and objective paradigm. Instead of objecting in seemingly idiosyncratic terms, the teacher can say, in effect, "Here's the reason, and it has nothing to do with you personally; on these specific grounds, you can see for yourself."

By the same token, the models begin to provide a means to forestall the deadening student rejoinder to teacher criticism, "Everyone gets it but you,"—referring, of course, to inferential connections among sentences that are obscure only to the pedantic English teacher. Not only do these models incorporate reader response in general and reader inferencing in particular; they identify specific conditions for allowable inference chains, specific strategies for appropriate placement of inference chains, and specific means for evaluating and controlling those chains.

As explicit editing devices, the patterns provide students with specific means for checking the cohesion of their work before turning it in. No student deliberately writes a noncohesive paper; by the time she finishes, she thinks she has achieved cohesion. If she is given patterns as an editing check-list, she has visible criteria which in turn can replace doubt and uncertainty with the satisfaction of having mastered a precise skill.

In their several roles as generative, evaluative, and editing devices, the patterns provide formal guidance to teachers and students, and at the same time a welcome breath of freedom. The fact that the patterns are derived from published texts in which there are many paragraphs without topic sentences can free the inexperienced teacher from the strangling grip and deadening pedagogy of the topic sentence. Students do read, and they notice lively, cohesive paragraphs without topic sentences, which can only leave them depressed by the lack of connection between their composition course and any real world writing they may be asked to do. The patterns provide the means for constructing and evaluating paragraphs without topic sentences.

After suggesting the various advantages that might accrue to those who use these models—and I think of them as advantages only, not as the kind of panacea many teachers want to make out of sentence-combining or linguistics in general—let me suggest briefly a three-stage introduction of the models into the classroom. The first task, obviously, is to identify them: in my own classes I use most of the sample paragraphs discussed in the analysis as examples of the various possible patterns. The second task is to introduce more samples for classroom discussion and exercises. The purpose here is to help the students see alternative arrangements of materials, along with the semantic and rhetorical implications of those arrangements, where before they saw none. The third task is to ask the students to rewrite inefficiently designed paragraphs and thus to demonstrate that they can not only recognize the patterns but can execute them as well.

Finally, I want to suggest that in whatever teaching capacity the models are used, they reflect the current—and, I believe, accurate—views of rhetoricians and discourse analysts. The models assume discourse to be a process, not a product, an interaction between individuals that requires the alert and attentive application of shared and informing structures to bridge the gaps in world knowledge between the writer and the reader.

Discourse Metaphors

While most systems of discourse analysis use the metaphor of a tree (whether explicitly or implicitly) to describe discourse structure, the analysis here suggests the metaphor of a systems network. The network consists of the whole text, made up of dominant terms (or nodes) which are introduced, explicated, and connected with other terms (or nodes) through the relationships established by syntactic and semantic dominance. The particular selection of these terms and relationships is governed by the communicative function of the text as a whole. Communicative function determines the complexity of the topic to be developed—whether by single, double, or combination recurrence chains—and also the amount of world knowledge that is assumed to be shared by author and reader. Seen as a network, discourse structure involves a system of interdependent components and "not merely . . . a hierarchy of lower-level units or . . . a one-dimensional linear concatenation," as implied by the metaphor of a tree hierarchy based exclusively on subordination.[5]

Whether the metaphor of a network can withstand further scrutiny remains to be seen. But to the extent that it can explain demonstrably functional structures (without pretending that these structures fully account for cohesion), and to the extent that it can identify the necessary interface between people and world knowledge, it can perhaps take us a step further in understanding the patterns that underlie all discourse. It enables us to see these patterns as distillations rather than reductions—distillations analogous to a person's perception of a shape on a page that allows her to say that this shape is an "a" not an "o", but also allows her to say that this "a" is more elegant than that "a".

Notes
Bibliography

Notes

1. Basic Notions

1. M. A. K. Halliday and Ruqaiya Hasan, *Cohesion in English* (London: Longmans, 1976), 10.
2. Stephen P. Witte and Lester Faigley, "Coherence, Cohesion, and Writing Quality," *College Composition and Communication* 32 (May 1981): 189–204.
3. Typical propositional research includes: Walter Kintsch, *The Representation of Meaning in Memory* (New York: Wiley, 1974); Gail McKoon, "Organization of Information in Text Memory," *Journal of Verbal Learning and Verbal Behavior* 16 (1977): 147–60.

2. The Cohesive Paragraph

1. E. V. Padučeva, "On the Structure of the Paragraph," *Linguistics* 131 (1974): 49.
2. Alexander Bain, *English Composition and Rhetoric* (London: Longmans, Green, and Co., 1877), 109.
3. Ibid., 116.
4. E. K. Lybbert and D. W. Cummings, "On Repetition and Coherence," *College Composition and Communication* 20 (1969): 35.
5. James McCrimmon, *Writing with a Purpose*, 4th ed. (New York: Houghton, 1967), 122.
6. John Hodges and Mary E. Whitten, *Harbrace College Handbook*, 5th ed. (New York: Harcourt, 1962), 328.

7. Charles Ruhl, "Prerequisites for a Linguistic Description of Coherence," *Language Science* 25 (1973): 15.
8. H. B. Lathrop, "Unity, Coherence, and Emphasis," *University of Wisconsin Studies in Language and Literature* 2 (1918): 82.
9. Lybbert and Cummings, 35.
10. Hodges and Whitten, 332.
11. Ibid., 333.
12. P. Joseph Canavan, *Paragraphs and Themes* (Lexington, Mass.: Heath, 1975), 71.
13. Herbert Zim, *Rocks and Minerals* (New York: Golden Pr., 1957), 71.
14. Irena Bellert, "On a Condition of the Coherence of Texts," *Semiotica* 2 (1970): 337.
15. Walter Kintsch and Douglas Vipond, "Reading Comprehension and Readability in Educational Practice and Psychological Theory" (Paper presented at the Conference on Memory, Univ. of Upsala, June 1977), 21.
16. Teun A. Van Dijk, "Text Grammar and Text Logic," in *Studies in Text Grammar*, ed. J. S. Petöfi and H. Rieser (Boston: Reidel Pub., 1973), 51.
17. Nils Erik Enkvist, *Linguistic Stylistics* (The Hague: Mouton, 1973), 117–18.
18. M. A. K. Halliday, "Linguistic Study of Texts," cited by William O. Hendricks, "On the Notion 'Beyond the Sentence,'" *Linguistics* 37 (1965): 22.
19. John Winburne, "Sentence Sequence in Discourse," cited by William O. Hendricks, "On the Notion 'Beyond the Sentence,'" *Linguistics* 37 (1965): 22.
20. Halliday and Hasan, 88–89.
21. Ibid., 31.
22. Ibid., 88.
23. Ibid., 143.
24. Ibid., 10.
25. Alvin Toffler, *Future Shock* (New York: Bantam, 1971), 126.
26. Robert M. Gorrell and Charlton Laird, eds., *Modern English Handbook*, 6th ed. (Englewood Cliffs, N.J.: Prentice-Hall, 1976), 125.
27. Ibid., 126.
28. McCrimmon, 122.
29. Louis T. Milic, *Stylists on Style: A Handbook with Selections for Analysis*, cited by Nils Erik Enkvist, *Linguistic Stylistics* (The Hague: Mouton, 1973), 123.
30. W. Ross Winterowd, "The Grammar of Coherence," *College English* 31 (1970).

31. W. Ross Winterowd, *The Contemporary Writer: A Practical Rhetoric* (New York: Harcourt, 1975), 113.
32. Hodges and Whitten, 328–29.
33. Lathrop, 82.
34. Geoffrey Leech, "'This Bread I Break'—Language and Interpretation," *A Review of English Literature* 6 (1965): 66.
35. Winterowd, "Grammar of Coherence," 828.
36. Jonathan Culler, *Structuralist Poetics: Structuralism, Linguistics, and the Study of Literature* (Ithaca, N.Y.: Cornell Univ. Pr., 1975), 91.
37. Ibid., 174.
38. Kenneth Burke, "The Nature of Form," in *Contemporary Rhetoric: A Conceptual Background with Readings*, ed. W. Ross Winterowd (New York: Harcourt, 1975), 183.
39. Ibid., 184.
40. Ibid.

3. The Reader and Cohesion

1. Culler, 171.
2. Roy O. Freedle and John B. Carroll, "Language Comprehension and the Acquisition of Knowledge: Reflections," in *Language Comprehension and the Acquisition of Knowledge*, ed. Roy O. Freedle and John B. Carroll (Washington, D.C.: Wiley, 1972), 361.
3. Ibid.
4. Randolf Quirk et al., *A Grammar of Contemporary English* (New York: Seminar Pr., 1974), 655–56.
5. A. L. Blumenthal, cited by John D. Bransford and Marcia K. Johnson, "Considerations of Some Problems of Comprehension," in *Visual Information Processing*, ed. William Chase (New York: Academic Pr., 1973), 421.
6. Bonnie Lynn Webber, *A Formal Approach to Discourse Anaphora* (New York: Garland Pub., 1979), v–1.
7. John D. Bransford, J. Barclay, and Jeffrey Franks, "Sentence Memory: A Cognitive Approach versus an Interpretative Approach," *Cognitive Psychology* 3 (1972): 207.
8. Susan E. Haviland and Herbert H. Clark, "What's New? Acquiring New Information as a Process in Comprehension," *Journal of Verbal Learning and Verbal Behavior* 13 (1974).
9. Perry W. Thorndyke, "The Role of Inference in Discourse Comprehension," *Journal of Verbal Learning and Verbal Behavior* 15 (1976): 438.
10. The distinction between lexical and world knowledge in this division is

admittedly a shadowy one. Bolinger questions the existence of any distinction between "knowledge of language" formalized by semantic markers and "knowledge of the world" (Dwight Bolinger, "The Atomization of Meaning," *Language* 41 [1965]: 555–73). Wilson comments: "There is no sharp line between what properly belongs in a dictionary and what properly belongs in an encyclopedia" (N. L. Wilson, "Linguistic Butter and Philosophical Parsnips," *Journal of Philosophy* 64 [1967]: 63). Undoubtedly, categorizing knowledge is a complicated affair, but examples do exist that suggest the validity of two separate categories. Katz provides one such example with his analysis of the following three sentences:

Bachelors are male.

Bachelors are not married.

Bachelors are over one inch tall.

As Katz points out, readers' rejections of the negations of sentences one and two are based on the lexical definition of bachelor, but rejection of sentence three's negation has nothing to do with one's sense of bachelorhood (J. J. Katz, *Semantic Theory* [New York: Harper, 1972], 72).

11. Van Dijk, 50.
12. Ibid.
13. Frank R. Yekovich and Carol H. Walker, "Identifying and Using Referents in Sentence Comprehension," *Journal of Verbal Learning and Verbal Behavior* 17 (1978).
14. Haviland and Clark.
15. Irena Bellert, "Solutions of the Problem of Presuppositions," in *Studies in Text Grammar*, ed. J. S. Petöfi and H. Rieser (Boston: Reidel Pub., 1973).
16. Walter Kintsch and D. Monk, "Storage of Complex Information in Memory: Some Implications of the Speed with which Inferences Can Be Made," *Journal of Experimental Psychology* 94 (1972).
17. Ruhl, 15.
18. Ibid.
19. Lawrence T. Frase, "Maintenance and Control in the Acquisition of Knowledge from Written Materials," in *Language Comprehension and the Acquisition of Knowledge*, ed. Roy O. Freedle and John B. Carroll (Washington, D.C.: Wiley, 1972).
20. Lawrence T. Frase, "Paragraph Organization of Written Materials: The Influence of Conceptual Clustering upon the Level and Organization of Recall," *Journal of Educational Psychology* 60 (1969).
21. Edward J. Crothers, "Memory and the Recall of Discourse," in *Lan-*

guage Comprehension and the Acquisition of Knowledge, ed. Roy O. Freedle and John B. Carroll (Washington, D.C.: Wiley, 1972), 273.

22. E. Charniak, cited by Marvin Minsky, "A Framework for Representing Knowledge," in *The Psychology of Computer Vision*, ed. P. Winston (New York: McGraw, 1975), 241.

23. I. M. Schlesinger, *Production and Comprehension of Utterances* (Hillsdale, N.J.: L. Erlbaum Assocs., 1977), 153.

24. D. E. Rumelhart, cited by Roger C. Schank and Robert P. Abelson, *Scripts, Plans, Goals and Understanding* (New York: Wiley, 1974), 10.

25. John D. Bransford and Marcia K. Johnson, "Considerations of Some Problems of Comprehension," 412.

26. A. Collins, J. S. Brown, and K. Larkin, cited by Webber, v–2.

27. Ibid.

28. R. Rommetveit, *On Message Structure: A Framework for the Study of Language and Communication* (New York: Wiley, 1974), 29.

29. Ibid.

30. Schlesinger, *Comprehension of Utterances*, 139.

31. Ibid., 138.

32. Kintsch, *Meaning in Memory*.

33. W. Ross Winterowd, "Syntax, Readability, Intention, and the Real World," *The Journal of English Teaching Techniques* 10 (1980): 23.

34. Tom Trabasso, "Mental Operations in Language Comprehension," in *Language Comprehension and the Acquisition of Knowledge*, ed. Roy O. Freedle and John B. Carroll (Washington, D.C.: Wiley, 1972).

35. I. M. Schlesinger, "Why a Sentence in which a Sentence in which a Sentence is Embedded is Embedded is Difficult," *Journal of Psycholinguistics* 4 (1975): 53–66.

36. Walter Kintsch and Janet Keenan, "Reading Rate and Retention as a Function of the Number of Propositions in the Base Structure of Sentences," *Cognitive Psychology* 5 (1973).

37. Harriet Salata Waters, "Superordinate-Subordinate Structure in Semantic Memory: The Roles of Comprehension and Retrieval Processes," *Journal of Verbal Learning and Verbal Behavior* 17 (1978).

38. McKoon, 148.

39. Ibid.

40. John D. Bransford and Jeffery Franks, "The Abstraction of Linguistic Ideas," *Cognitive Psychology* 2 (1971): 331.

41. Crothers, 247–83.

42. Charles Perfetti and Susan R. Goldman, "Thematization and Sentence Retrieval," *Journal of Verbal Learning and Verbal Behavior* 13 (1974): 71.

43. Frantisek Daneš, in Enkvist, 120–21.

44. Stephen Tyler, *The Said and the Unsaid: Mind, Meaning and Culture* (New York: Academic Pr., 1978), 378.

4. Single Term Paragraphs

1. Walter Davis, *The Act of Interpretation: A Critique of Literary Reason* (Chicago: Univ. of Chicago Pr., 1978), 1.
2. Bain, 116.
3. Paul Rogers, "Alexander Bain and the Rise of the Organic Paragraph," *Quarterly Journal of Speech* 51 (1965): 404.
4. James McConkey, cited by Paul Rogers, "A Discourse-Centered Rhetoric of the Paragraph," *College Composition and Communication* 17 (1966): 4.
5. Leo Rockas, *Modes of Rhetoric* (New York: St. Martin, 1964), 4.
6. Arthur Stern, "When is a Paragraph?" *College Composition and Communication* 27 (1976): 253.
7. Richard Braddock, "The Frequency and Placement of Topic Sentences in Expository Prose," *Research in the Teaching of English* 8 (1974): 299.
8. Frank Koen, Alton Becker, Richard Young, "The Pyschological Reality of the Paragraph," *Proceedings of the Conference on Language and Language Behavior*, ed. Eric M. Zale (New York: Appleton, 1968), 178.
9. Francis Christensen, "A Generative Rhetoric of the Paragraph," in *Teaching Freshman Composition*, ed. Gary Tate and Edward P. J. Corbett (New York: Oxford Univ. Pr., 1967), 205.
10. Halliday and Hasan, 10–11.
11. Truman Capote, *Other Voices, Other Rooms* (New York: Vintage Books, 1948), 9.
12. Halliday and Hasan, 297.
13. *Time*, "The Euphemism: Telling It Like It Isn't," in *Language Awareness*, ed. Paul A. Eschholz, Alfred F. Rosa, and Virginia Clark (New York: St. Martin, 1974), 18.
14. Roland Barthes, cited by Culler, 220.
15. John Erskine, cited by Francis Christensen, *Notes Toward a New Rhetoric* (New York: Harper, 1967), 25.
16. *Time*, 17.
17. Roland Barthes, cited by Culler, 219.
18. N. Scott Momaday, "The Way to Rainy Mountain," in *A Writer's Reader*, ed. Donald Hall and D. L. Emblen (Boston: Little, 1976), 18.
19. Barbara Tuchman, "History as Mirror," in *A Writer's Reader*, ed. Donald Hall and D. L. Emblen (Boston: Little, 1976), 27.
20. Paul Stevens, "Weasel Words: God's Little Helpers," in *Language*

Awareness, ed. Paul A. Eschholz, Alfred F. Rosa, and Virginia Clark (New York: St. Martin, 1974), 156.

21. Susanne K. Langer, cited by Harry Crosby and George F. Estey, *College Writing* (New York: Harper, 1968), 108.

22. Otto Friedrich, "A Vivacious Blonde Was Fatally Shot or How to Read a Tabloid," in *Language Awareness*, ed. Paul A. Eschholz, Alfred F. Rosa, and Virginia Clark (New York: St. Martin, 1974), 194.

23. Culler, 220.

24. A. L. Becker, "A Tagmemic Approach to Paragraph Analysis," *College Composition and Communication* 16 (1965): 237–48; Christensen, "Generative Rhetoric of the Paragraph," 200–16.

5. Multiple Chain Paragraphs

1. Braddock, 293.
2. Willy Ley, cited by Gorrell and Laird, 126.
3. William G. Moulton, cited by Francis Christensen and Bonniejean Christensen, *A New Rhetoric* (New York: Harper, 1976), 144.
4. E. D. Hirsch, Jr., *The Philosophy of Composition* (Chicago: Univ. of Chicago Pr., 1977), 109.
5. Culler, 171.
6. Frantisek Daneš, cited by Enkvist, 120.
7. *The Techno/Peasant* Survival Manual* (New York: Bantam, 1980), 9.
8. Edward T. Hall, *The Hidden Dimension* (Garden City, N.Y.: Anchor Books, 1969), 13.

6. Implications and Applications

1. Walter Kintsch, *Meaning in Memory*, 14.
2. Kintsch and Vipond, 45–47.
3. Francis Christensen, "A Generative Rhetoric of the Paragraph," in *Notes Toward a New Rhetoric* (New York: Harper, 1967), 60.
4. Christensen, "Generative Rhetoric of the Paragraph"; Paul Rogers, "Discourse-Centered Rhetoric of the Paragraph."
5. Ursula Oomen, "New Models and Methods in Text Analysis," *Report of the Twenty-Second Round Table Meeting on Linguistics and Language Studies*, ed. Richard J. O'Brien (Washington, D.C.: Georgetown Univ. Pr., 1971), 216.

Bibliography

Bain, Alexander. *English Composition and Rhetoric.* London: Longmans, 1877.

Barthes, Roland. Cited by Jonathan Culler, *Structuralist Poetics: Structuralism, Linguistics, and the Study of Literature.* Ithaca, N.Y.: Cornell Univ. Pr., 1975.

Becker, A. L. "A Tagmemic Approach to Paragraph Analysis." *College Composition and Communication* 16 (1965): 237–74.

Bellert, Irena. "On a Condition of the Coherence of Texts." *Semiotica* 2 (1970): 335–63.

————. "Solutions of the Problem of Presuppositions." In *Studies in Text Grammar*, edited by J. S. Petöfi and H. Rieser, 79–95. Boston: Riedel Pub., 1973.

Blumenthal, A. L. Cited by John D. Bransford and Marcia K. Johnson, "Considerations of Some Problems of Comprehension." In *Visual Information Processing*, edited by William Chase, 383–438. New York: Academic Pr., 1973.

Bolinger, Dwight. "The Atomization of Meaning." *Language* 41 (1965): 555–77.

Braddock, Richard. "The Frequency and Placement of Topic Sentences in Expository Prose." *Research in the Teaching of English* 8 (1974): 287–302.

Bransford, John D., and Marcia K. Johnson. "Considerations of Some Problems of Comprehension." In *Visual Information Processing*, edited by William Chase, 383–438. New York: Academic Pr., 1973.

Bransford, John D., J. Barclay and Jeffery Franks. "Sentence Memory: A Cognitive Approach versus an Interpretative Approach." *Cognitive Psychology* 3 (1972): 193–209.

Bransford, John D., and Jeffery Franks. "The Abstraction of Linguistic Ideas." *Cognitive Psychology* 2 (1971): 331–50.

Burke, Kenneth. "The Nature of Form." In *Contemporary Rhetoric: A Conceptual Background with Readings*, edited by W. Ross Winterowd, 183–99. New York: Harcourt, 1975.

Canavan, P. Joseph. *Paragraphs and Themes*. Lexington, Mass.: Heath, 1975.

Capote, Truman. *Other Voices, Other Rooms*. New York: Vintage Books, 1948.

Charniak, E. Cited by Marvin Minsky, "A Framework for Representing Knowledge." In *The Psychology of Computer Vision*, edited by P. Winston, 211–77. New York: McGraw, 1975.

Christensen, Francis. "A Generative Rhetoric of the Paragraph." In *Teaching Freshman Composition*, edited by Gary Tate and Edward P. J. Corbett, 200–16. New York: Oxford Univ. Pr., 1967.

———. *Notes Toward a New Rhetoric*. New York: Harper, 1967.

Collins, A., J. S. Brown, and K. Larkin. Cited by Bonnie Lynn Webber, *A Formal Approach to Discourse Anaphora*. New York: Garland Pub., 1979.

Crothers, Edward J. "Memory and the Recall of Discourse." In *Language Comprehension and the Acquisition of Knowledge*, edited by Roy O. Freedle and John B. Carroll, 247–83. Washington, D.C.: Wiley, 1972.

Culler, Jonathan. *Structuralist Poetics: Structuralism, Linguistics, and the Study of Literature*. Ithaca, N.Y.: Cornell Univ. Pr., 1975.

Daneš, Frantisek. Cited by Nils Erik Enkvist, *Linguistic Stylistics*. The Hague: Mouton, 1973.

Davis. Walter. *The Act of Interpretation: A Critique of Literary Reason*. Chicago: Univ. of Chicago Pr., 1978.

Enkvist, Nils Erik. *Linguistic Stylistics*. The Hague: Mouton, 1973.

Erskine, John. Cited by Francis Christensen, *Notes Toward a New Rhetoric*. New York: Harper, 1967.

Frase, Lawrence T. "Maintenance and Control in the Acquisition of Knowledge from Written Materials." In *Language Comprehension and the Acquisition of Knowledge*, edited by Roy O. Freedle and John B. Carroll, 337–56. Washington, D.C.: Wiley, 1972.

Frase, Lawrence T. "Paragraph Organization of Written Materials: The Influence of Conceptual Clustering upon the Level and Organization of Recall." *Journal of Educational Psychology* 60 (1969): 394–401.

Freedle, Roy O., and John B. Carroll, eds. *Language Comprehension and the Acquisition of Knowledge.* Washington, D.C.: Wiley, 1972.

Friedrich, Otto. "A Vivacious Blonde Was Fatally Shot or How to Read a Tabloid." In *Language Awareness,* edited by Paul A. Eschholz, Alfred F. Rosa, and Virginia Clark, 193–99. New York: St. Martin, 1974.

Gorrell, Robert M., and Charlton Laird, eds. *Modern English Handbook.* 6th ed. Englewood Cliffs, N.J.: Prentice-Hall, 1976.

Hall, Edward T. *The Hidden Dimension.* Garden City, N.Y.: Anchor Books, 1969.

Halliday, M. A. K. "Linguistic Study of Texts." Cited by William O. Hendricks, "On the Notion 'Beyond the Sentence.'" *Linguistics* 37 (1965): 12–57.

Halliday, M. A. K., and Ruqaiya Hasan. *Cohesion in English.* London: Longmans, 1976.

Haviland, Susan E., and Herbert H. Clark. "What's New? Acquiring New Information as a Process in Comprehension." *Journal of Verbal Learning and Verbal Behavior* 13 (1974): 512–21.

Hendricks, William O. "On the Notion 'Beyond the Sentence.'" *Linguistics* 37 (1965): 12–57.

Hirsch, E. D., Jr. *The Philosophy of Composition.* Chicago: Univ. of Chicago Pr., 1977.

Hodges, John, and Mary E. Whitten. *Harbrace College Handbook.* 5th ed. New York: Harcourt, 1962.

Katz, J. J. *Semantic Theory.* New York: Harper, 1972.

Kintsch, Walter. *The Representation of Meaning in Memory.* New York: Wiley, 1974.

Kintsch, Walter, and Janet Keenan. "Reading Rate and Retention as a Function of the Number of Propositions in the Base Structure of Sentences." *Cognitive Psychology* 5 (1973): 257–74.

Kintsch, Walter, and D. Monk. "Storage of Complex Information in Memory: Some Implications of the Speed with which Inferences Can Be Made." *Journal of Experimental Psychology* 94 (1972): 25–32.

Kintsch, Walter, and Douglas Vipond. "Reading Comprehension and Readability in Educational Practice and Psychological Theory." Paper presented at the Conference on Memory, Univ. of Upsala, June 1977.

Koen, Frank, Alton Becker, and Richard Young. "The Psychological Reality of the Paragraph." *Proceedings of the Conference on Language and Language Behavior*, edited by Eric M. Zale. New York: Appleton, 1968.

Langer, Susanne K. Cited by Harry Crosby and George F. Estey, *College Writing*. New York: Harper, 1968.

Lathrop, H. B. "Unity, Coherence, and Emphasis." *University of Wisconsin Studies in Language and Literature* 2 (1918): 77–98.

Leech, Geoffrey. "'This Bread I Break'—Language and Interpretation." *A Review of English Literature* 6 (1965): 66–75.

Ley, Willy. Cited by Robert M. Gorrell and Charlton Laird, *Modern English Handbook*. 6th ed. Englewood Cliffs, N.J.: Prentice-Hall, 1976.

Lybbert, E. K., and D. W. Cummings. "On Repetition and Coherence." *College Composition and Communication* 20 (1969): 35–38.

McConkey, James. Cited by Paul Rogers, "A Discourse-Centered Rhetoric of the Paragraph." *College Composition and Communication* 17 (1966): 2–11.

McCrimmon, James. *Writing with a Purpose*. 4th ed. New York: Houghton, 1967.

McKoon, Gail. "Organization of Information in Text Memory." *Journal of Verbal Learning and Verbal Behavior* 16 (1977): 147–60.

Milic, Louis T. *Stylists on Style: A Handbook with Selections for Analysis.* Cited by Nils Erik Enkvist, *Linguistic Stylistics*. The Hague: Mouton, 1973.

Momaday, N. Scott. "The Way to Rainy Mountain." In *A Writer's Reader*, edited by Donald Hall and D. L. Emblen, 18–23. Boston: Little, 1976.

Moulton, William G. Cited by Francis Christensen and Bonniejean Christensen, *A New Rhetoric*. New York: Harper, 1976.

Oomen, Ursula. "New Models and Methods in Text Analysis." *Report of the Twenty-Second Round Table Meeting on Linguistics and Language Studies*, edited by Richard J. O'Brien. Washington, D.C.: Georgetown Univ. Pr., 1971. 211–22.

Orwell, George. "'Such, Such Were the Joys . . .'" *A Collection of Essays*. Garden City, N.Y.: Anchor Books, 1954, 9–55.

Padučeva, E. V. "On the Structure of the Paragraph." *Linguistics* 131 (1974): 49–58.

Perfetti, Charles, and Susan R. Goldman. "Thematization and Sentence Retrieval." *Journal of Verbal Learning and Verbal Behavior* 13 (1974): 70–79.

Quirk, Randolf, Sidney Greenbaum, Geoffrey Leech, and Jan Svartvik. *A Grammar of Contemporary English.* New York: Seminar Pr., 1974.

Rockas, Leo. *Modes of Rhetoric.* New York: St. Martin, 1964.

Rogers, Paul. "Alexander Bain and the Rise of the Organic Paragraph." *Quarterly Journal of Speech* 51 (1965): 298–308.

————. "A Discourse-Centered Rhetoric of the Paragraph," *College Composition and Communication* 17 (1966): 2–11.

Rommetveit, R. *On Message Structure: A Framework for the Study of Language and Communication.* New York: Wiley, 1974.

Ruhl, Charles. "Prerequisties for a Linguistic Description of Coherence." *Language Science* 25 (1973): 15–18.

Rumelhart, D. E. Cited by Roger C. Schank and Robert P. Abelson, *Scripts, Plans, Goals and Understanding.* New York: Wiley, 1977.

Schlesinger, I. M. *Production and Comprehension of Utterances.* Hillsdale, N.J.: L. Erlbaum Assocs., 1977.

————. "Why a Sentence in which a Sentence in which a Sentence is Embedded is Embedded is Difficult." *Journal of Psycholinguistics* 4 (1975): 53–66.

Stern, Arthur. "When Is a Paragraph?" *College Composition and Communication* 27 (1976): 253–57.

Stevens, Paul. "Weasel Words: God's Little Helpers," In *Language Awareness*, edited by Paul A. Eschholz, Alfred F. Rosa, and Virginia Clark, 155–71. New York: St. Martin, 1974.

The Techno/Peasant* Survival Manual. New York: Bantam, 1980.

Thorndyke, Perry W. "The Role of Inference in Discourse Comprehension." *Journal of Verbal Learning and Verbal Behavior* 15 (1976): 437–46.

Time. "The Euphemism: Telling It Like It Isn't." In *Language Awareness*, edited by Paul A. Eschholz, Alfred F. Rosa, and Virginia Clark, 16–21. New York: St. Martin, 1974.

Toffler, Alvin. *Future Shock.* New York: Bantam, 1971.

Trabasso, Tom. "Mental Operations in Language Comprehension." In *Language Comprehension and the Acquisition of Knowledge*, edited by Roy O. Freedle and John B. Carroll, 113–37. Washington, D.C.: Wiley, 1972.

Tuchman, Barbara. "History as Mirror." In *A Writer's Reader*, edited by Donald Hall and D. L. Emblen, 25–38. Boston: Little, 1976.

Tyler, Stephen. *The Said and the Unsaid: Mind, Meaning and Culture.* New York: Academic Pr., 1978.

Van Dijk, Teun A. "Text Grammar and Text Logic." In *Studies in Text Grammar*, edited by J. S. Petöfi and H. Rieser, 17–74. Boston: Reidel Pub., 1973.

Waters, Harriet Salata. "Superordinate-Subordinate Structure in Semantic Memory: The Roles of Comprehension and Retrieval Processes." *Journal of Verbal Learning and Verbal Behavior* 17 (1978): 587–97.

Webber, Bonnie Lynn. *A Formal Approach to Discourse Anaphora*. New York: Garland Pub., 1979.

Wilson, N. L. "Linguistic Butter and Philosophical Parsnips." *Journal of Philosophy* 64 (1967): 55–67.

Winburne, John. "Sentence Sequence in Discourse." Cited by William O. Hendricks, "On the Notion 'Beyond the Sentence.'" *Linguistics* 37 (1965): 12–57.

Winterowd, W. Ross. *The Contemporary Writer: A Practical Rhetoric*. New York: Harcourt, 1975.

———. "The Grammar of Coherence." *College English* 31 (1970): 828–35.

———. "Syntax, Readability, Intention, and the Real World." *The Journal of English Teaching Techniques* 10 (1980): 21–31.

Witte, Stephen P., and Lester Faigley. "Coherence, Cohesion, and Writing Quality." *College Composition and Communication* 32 (May 1981): 189–204.

Yekovich, Frank R., and Carol H. Walker. "Identifying and Using Referents in Sentence Comprehension." *Journal of Verbal Learning and Verbal Behavior* 17 (1978): 265–77.

Zim, Herbert. *Rocks and Minerals*. New York: Golden Pr., 1957.